ALSO BY CHUCK KLOSTERMAN

Fargo Rock City:
A Heavy Metal Odyssey in Rural Nörth Daköta

Sex, Drugs, and Cocoa Puffs:
A Low Culture Manifesto

Killing Yourself to Live:
85% of a True Story

Chuck Klosterman IV:
A Decade of Curious People and Dangerous Ideas

Downtown Owl:
A Novel

Eating the Dinosaur

The Visible Man:
A Novel

I WEAR THE BLACK HAT

GRAPPLING WITH VILLAINS
(REAL AND IMAGINED)

CHUCK KLOSTERMAN

SCRIBNER

New York   London   Toronto   Sydney   New Delhi

SCRIBNER
A Division of Simon & Schuster, Inc.
1230 Avenue of the Americas
New York, NY 10020

First Scribner hardcover edition July 2013

DESIGNED BY ERICH HOBBING

Manufactured in the United States of America

1   3   5   7   9   10   8   6   4   2

Library of Congress Control Number: 2013003049

ISBN 978-1-4391-8449-3
ISBN 978-1-4391-8451-6 (ebook)

One should judge a man mainly from his depravities.
Virtues can be faked. Depravities are real.

—Klaus Kinski, super nihilist.

I'm gonna quote a line from Yeats, I think it is: "The
best lack all conviction, while the best are filled" . . .
oh, no. It's the other way around. "The best lack all
conviction, and the *worst* are filled with a passionate
intensity." Now, you figure out where I am.

—Lou Reed, super high.

I'm not a good guy. I mean, I don't hurt anybody. But
I don't help, either.

—Louis C.K., super real.

CONTENTS

I WEAR THE
BLACK HAT

PREFACE

It seems like twenty-five lifetimes ago, but it was only twenty-five years: An older friend gave me a cassette he'd duplicated from a different cassette (it was the era of "tape dubbing," which was like file sharing for iguanodons). It was a copy of an album I'd wanted, but the album was only thirty-eight minutes long; that meant there were still seven open minutes at the end of the cassette's A-side. In order to fill the gap, my friend included an extra song by Metallica. It was a cover of a song by the British band Diamond Head, a group I was completely unfamiliar with. The opening lines of the song deeply disturbed me, mostly because I misinterpreted their meaning (although I suspect the guys in Metallica did, too). The lyrics described bottomless vitriol toward the songwriter's mother and a desire to burn her alive. The chorus was malicious and straightforward: *"Am I evil? Yes I am. Am I evil? I am man."*

I can't remember precisely what I thought when I first heard those words—I was a teenager, so it was probably something creative and contradictory, and I'm relatively positive I imagined a nonexistent comma after the fourth *am*. But I do remember how I felt. I was confused and I was interested. And if I could have explained my mental state at fourteen with the clarity of language I have as a forty-year-old, I assume my reaction would have been the same complicated question I ask myself today: Why would anyone *want* to be evil?

* * *

1

I am typing this sentence on an autumn afternoon. The leaves are all dead, but still tethered to the trees, waiting for a colder future. Outside my living room window and three floors below, people are on the street. I vaguely recognize some of them, but not most of them. I rarely remember the names or faces of nonfictional people. Still, I believe these strangers are nonthreatening. I suppose you never know for certain what unfamiliar humans are like, but I'm confident. They are more like me than they are different: predominantly white, in the vicinity of middle age, and dressed in a manner that suggests a different social class than the one they truly occupy (most appear poorer than they actually are, but a few skew in the opposite direction). Everyone looks superficially friendly, but none are irrefutably trustworthy. And as I watch these people from my window, I find myself wondering something:

Do I care about any of them?

I certainly don't dislike them, because I have no reason to do so. If one of these strangers were suddenly in trouble and I had the ability to help, I absolutely would—but I suspect my motive for doing so might not be related to *them*. I think it would be the result of all the social obligations I've been ingrained to accept, or perhaps to protect my own self-identity, or maybe because I'd feel like a coward if I didn't help a damaged person in public (or maybe because others might see me actively ignoring a person in need). I care about strangers when they're abstractions, but I feel almost nothing when they're literally in front of me. They seem like unnamed characters in a poorly written novel about myself, which was written poorly by me. The perspective is first person, but the hero doesn't do much. He doesn't do anything. He just looks out the window.

This realization makes me feel shame . . . yet not so ashamed that I suddenly (and authentically) care about random people on the street. I feel worse about myself, but I feel no differently about them. And this prompts me to consider several questions at once:

1) Am I a psychopath?

2) Is my definition of the word *care* different from the definition held by other people? Is it possible that I *do* care, but that I define "caring" as an all-encompassing, unrealistic aspiration (so much so that it makes it impossible for me to recognize my own empathy)?

3) Does my awareness of this emotional gap actually mean I care *more* than other people? Or is that comical self-deception?

4) What if these strangers are bad people? Would that eliminate my emotional responsibility? Nobody needs to feel bad about not caring about Adolf Hitler. Right? Right. Well, what if some of these anonymous strangers—if given the means and opportunity—might behave exactly like Hitler? Or worse than Hitler? What if one of these people would become the Super Hitler, if granted unlimited power? Do I have to care about them until they prove otherwise? Do I have to care about them as humans *until* they invade Poland? And in order to be truly good, do I still need to keep caring about them even after they've done so?

5) Why do I always suspect everyone is lying about how they feel?

6) Why do I think I can understand the world by staring out the window?

7) Let's assume half the people on my street are categorically "good" and half are categorically "bad." I can't tell who is who, but (somehow) I know that this is irrefutably the case. Let's also operate from the position that humans somehow have agency over those two classifications. Let's assume there is no Higher Power and no afterlife, and that all of these self-aware people—regardless of their social history or familial upbringing—are able to *decide* if they want to be good or bad. Let's assume it's every human's unambiguous choice, based on all the information available. If this is

true, then the import of the word "good" and the import of the word "bad" are nothing more than constructions. They are classifications we created subjectively; their meanings don't derive from any larger reality or any deeper truth. They're just the two definitions we have *agreed* upon, based on various books and myths and parables and philosophies and artworks and whatever "feels" like the innate difference between rightness and wrongness. In other words, there are "good people" and there are "bad people," but those two designations are unreal. The designations exist in conversation, but they're utterly made-up. Within this scenario, would goodness still be something to aspire to? Wouldn't this mean that good people are simply the ones who accept that what they've been told is arbitrarily true? That they've accepted a policy they didn't create for themselves?

8) American philosopher John Rawls (1921–2002) had a lot of mind-crushing ideas, but perhaps the most significant was his concept of "the veil of ignorance." It best applies to the creation of social contracts. At risk of oversimplification, Rawls's scenario was basically this: Let's pretend you were instantly able to re-create American society in totality, and you could do it in whatever way you wanted. You could make (or eliminate) whatever laws you desired, and you could implement whatever financial and judicial structures you believed would work best. However, you must do this under a magical "veil of ignorance." The moment after you create this system, you'll no longer be yourself (and you don't have any idea what your new role in this society shall be). You might be a rough facsimile of your current self, or you might be someone entirely new. Your gender might be different, or your race. It's possible you will be extremely destitute and appallingly ugly. You'll have a different level of intelligence and a different work ethic. You might suddenly be disabled, or super athletic, or homosex-

ual, or criminally insane. As such, you will (probably) want to create a society that is as fair and complete as possible, since you have no idea what station you'll inherit within your own new, self-constructed boundaries. You need to think outside of your current self, because tomorrow you'll be someone else entirely. But try that same process with *goodness*, and particularly with how we gauge what goodness is. Try to come up with a list of declarations or rules that outline a universal definition for what it means to be good, for all people, for the rest of time. And do this under another "veil of ignorance." Do this with the knowledge that—tomorrow—you will be a totally different person who views the world in a manner alien to your current self. This new you may have no ability to control your darker impulses. You may be incapable of natural compassion. You might have the emotional baggage of someone who was habitually ridiculed as a teenager, or of a child who was sexually tortured, or of a sorority girl born so rich she's never had a real chance to comprehend any life except the one she fell into by chance. Would this possibility affect your forthcoming invention of *goodness*? Would you define the concept more broadly and with greater elasticity? For some reason, it's human nature to say no. Our inclination is to see goodness as something that exists within itself; we want to believe goodness and badness are fundamental traits that transcend status or personal experience. The sorority girl and the serial killer don't get special dispensation due to circumstance. We do not want to see goodness and badness as things we *decide,* because those are terms that we need to be decided by someone else.

9) Am I evil? Yes. I am, man.

This book is about presentation. It seems like it should be about "context," but I've come to realize that audiences create context more than the creator. This book is about the *presentation* of material, since the posture of that presentation—more than what is technically and literally expressed—dictates the meaning that is (eventually) contextualized by others. Even if we view something as satire, we must first accept that a nonsatirical version of that argument exists for other people, even if they're people we've never met. If it didn't, why would we mock it? [This, I suppose, is a complicated way of explaining something too uncomfortable to state clearly: It's possible that context doesn't matter at all. It seems like it should matter deeply, because we've all been trained to believe "context is everything." But why do we believe that? It's because that phrase allows us to make things mean whatever we want, for whatever purpose we need.]

Here's what this book will not be: It will not be a 200-page comparison of the Beatles to the Rolling Stones, even though I was tempted to do so in seventeen different paragraphs. It will not analyze pro wrestling or women on reality TV shows who are not there to make friends. And most notably, it will not be a repetitive argument that insists every bad person is not-so-bad and every good person is not-so-good. Rational people already understand that this is how the world is. But if you are not-so-rational—if there are certain characters you simply refuse to think about in a manner that isn't 100 percent negative or 100 percent positive—parts of this book will (mildly) offend you. It will make you angry, and you will find yourself trying to intellectually discount arguments that you might naturally make about other people. This is what happens whenever the things we feel and the things we know refuse to align in the way we're conditioned to pretend.

Before I started this project, I had lunch with my editor (the same editor who eventually worked on this manuscript). We were talking about *Star Wars*, which his four-year-old son had recently watched for the first time. The boy was blown away. In the course of our conversation, I expressed my theory that there's a natural evolution to how male audiences respond to the *Star Wars* franchise: When you're very young, the character you love most is Luke Skywalker (who's entirely good). As you grow older, you gravitate toward Han Solo (who's ultimately good, but superficially bad). But by the time you reach adulthood, and when you hit the point in your life where *Star Wars* starts to seem like what it actually is (a better-than-average space opera containing one iconic idea), you inevitably find yourself relating to Darth Vader. As an adult, Vader is easily the most intriguing character, and seemingly the only essential one.

"I'm not sure all people would agree with your premise," said my editor. "I think most guys stop evolving at Han Solo."

That's when we started talking about this book, or what this book would theoretically be. Our conversation was nebulous. My editor wanted to know why I wanted to write about villains. I said I could not give a cogent explanation, but that I knew this was the book I wanted to write.

"Well, I have my own theory," he said. "I think I know why you want to do this. I think it's because you're afraid that you are actually a villainous person."

I had no response. Much later, I wrote this.

WHAT YOU SAY ABOUT
HIS COMPANY IS WHAT YOU SAY
ABOUT SOCIETY

What is the most villainous move on the market?

I suppose "murdering a bunch of innocent people" seems like the obvious answer, but it obviously isn't (there are countless statues of heroes who've killed thousands). Electrocuting helpless dogs for the sake of convenience seems almost as diabolical, but not diabolical enough to keep you off the NFL Pro Bowl roster. Rape is vile; human trafficking is disturbing; blowing up a planet and blotting out the sun are not for the innocent. These are all terrible, terrible things. Yet none of them represent the *pinnacle* of villainy. None of them embody culture's most sinister deed.

The most villainous move any person can make is tying a woman to the railroad tracks.

There's simply no confusion over the implication of this specific act: If you see someone tying a woman to train tracks, you are seeing an unadulterated expression of evil. Such a crime is not just the work of a villain, but of someone who wants to be a villainous cliché. In 2008, this actually happened in Thailand—a twenty-seven-year-old woman named Niparat Tawonporn was tied to a railway path about five hundred miles south of Bangkok and cut in half by the oncoming locomotive (it was rumored to be the result of some unexplained romantic disagree-

ment, although that was merely conjecture among the local vil-
lagers). Still, this kind of ritualistic homicide is exceedingly rare.
In response to the query "Did anyone really ever get tied to the
railroad tracks?," weirdness raconteur Cecil Adams (creator of
the wry "Straight Dope" column for the *Chicago Reader*) detailed
the following dossier: "The earliest real-life incident I could find
was from 1874, when on August 31 the *New York Times* reported
that a Frenchman named Gardner had been robbed and tied to
railroad tracks. He managed to loosen all the ropes but the one
that secured his left foot, and the train cut off his leg below the
knee. Though he survived to describe the attack, he soon died
of his injuries." The five other examples Adams cites include a
thirteen-year-old boy kidnapped in 1881 and a college student
from 1906 who experienced the worst nonsexual fraternity initia-
tion imaginable. All told, this is not much train-related violence,
particularly since all the victims mentioned were male. It's sexist
to say this, but—somehow—tying a *man* to the train tracks just
doesn't seem as wicked.

Considering its scarcity, it's unclear how a crime that almost
never happened became the definitive Crime Of The (Nineteenth) Century. Its origin is mostly a theatrical construction. The
first "popular" images of humans roped to railroad ties derived
from an 1863 British play titled *The Engineer* and an 1867 American play titled *Under the Gaslight*. By the dawn of the silent-movie
era, the trope had been adopted completely: The 1913 comedy
Barney Oldfield's Race for a Life is structured around a woman tied
to the tracks. Serials from 1914 like *The Hazards of Helen* and *The
Perils of Pauline* employed similar premises. But in those cases,
the idea is already comedic. It's satiric melodrama. It's almost as
if the concept of using a train to kill someone is so complicated
and absurd that it can only be viewed as a *caricature* of villainy.
It was never based on any legitimate fear. This is even true with
the first (and only?) pop song about train-related homicide, the
Coasters' 1959 single "Along Came Jones," in which a woman is

assaulted through a variety of bizarre, ever-escalating means, all in the hope of stealing the deed to her ranch.

This is why no nonfictional villain can compete with Snidely Whiplash.

Snidely Whiplash was the animated villain in the Dudley Do-Right segments of the 1960s cartoon *Rocky and Bullwinkle*. (Dudley was the dim-witted Canadian Mountie who was always trying to capture Snidely.) Based on the silent-movie villain archetype, Whiplash had a waxed mustache and a black hat (and, of course, is literally named "Snidely"). He spoke with a hiss and laughed like a maniac. However, his true failing was a compulsion. Snidely Whiplash was obsessed with tying women to railroad tracks. He simply couldn't stop himself. It was the foundation of his entire ethos. And this was what made him so amusing: his total inability to express any reason whatsoever as to why he was doing so. There didn't seem to be any financial upside or competitive advantage; Snidely Whiplash just enjoyed placing Canadian women in a position where they *wait* to die. He loved the idea of his victims hearing the chug-chug-chug of the machine that would kill them in the future, even though that sadistic lag time did not benefit him in any way (beyond giving him a few extra moments to stroke his mustache). There was no thinking behind his sadism; it was just something he did, seemingly every day of his cartoon life. He had no external purpose. His only motive for tying women to railroad tracks was that tying women to railroad tracks was what he did.

So we begin, I suppose, with a question: What's scarier—a villain with a motive, or a villain without one?

Machiavelli poses a problem for any historian hoping to reconcile the gap between personal psychology and social memory. He is both famous and unknown—a polarizing figure regularly referenced by people who know nothing about his existence, or even his first name. Born in Florence, Italy, in 1469, Niccolò Machiavelli had lived a relatively full life long before he did anything truly memorable: For fourteen years, he served as a key diplomat for his native city until he was (wrongly) accused of conspiracy against the Medici family government (who had come into power around 1512). Machiavelli was subsequently imprisoned and tortured by means of "the strappado." This was gravity-based brutality: The victim was hoisted into the air with both hands tied behind his back and repeatedly dropped onto a stone floor. Having nothing to confess, the forty-four-year-old Machiavelli was eventually exiled to a farm, where he became a writer (and the accidental inspiration for Tupac Shakur). Machiavelli died on June 22, 1527. Every so often, someone will suggest that he faked his own death, although that rumor exists only because it retrospectively seems like something Machiavelli would support.

The one thing we all collectively understand about Machiavelli is the eponym *Machiavellian,* a catch-all term for the attainment of power through cunning. It's almost a compliment, but only to an especially self-absorbed criminal (or, in the case of hip-hop, to those who aspire to a criminal reputation). This perception can be inferred through much of his writing catalog, although the only book that really matters is *The Prince,* a treatise on the dynamics of interpersonal relationships within the political sphere. It was published five years after the author had died. There are some undeniably radical ideas in *The Prince*; the ideas might seem self-evident in the present day, but they exploded minds in the sixteenth century. The biggest idea reconsiders the reality of motive: Throughout the Middle Ages and the Renaissance, monarchies operated (or at least pretended to operate) from a bizarrely optimistic perspective. They believed (or at least claimed to believe) that the best way for any ruler to succeed was through virtue; if the populace saw their leader as righteous and noble and pure, they would be more likely to support and follow him. To be a good king, you had to be a good person (or so the thinking went). *The Prince* argues that this kind of principle is ridiculous and naïve; instead, Machiavelli suggests that the essential key to attaining and holding power was *being powerful*. It's an umbrella philosophy that informs every detail. According to *The Prince*, the traditional definition of virtue is at best a nonfactor and potentially a detriment; to Machiavelli, the only true virtue is craft. Being feared is better than being loved. Laws are essential, but they're nothing more than constructions (and they work only if the populace cowers to the concept of state domination). Instead of allowing life to happen by chance, whatever one desires should be pursued and taken. If you have to slay a bunch of your enemies, do so on the first day of the job; that way, you'll seem nicer in the future (since killing will no longer be necessary). A prince "must not have any other object or any other thought, nor must he adopt anything as his art but war," the author plainly states.

Now, before I go any further, I need to note something important: It's entirely possible (and perhaps even probable) that Machiavelli was being sarcastic. In fact, that seems to be the ever-encroaching consensus. *The Prince* was very controversial for a very long time, but those who have studied the writer most tend to believe it was intended as a criticism of human nature. For example, Salman Rushdie adores Machiavelli and views him as a pragmatist: "I just think Machiavelli has been maligned by history," he said in 2008. "To put it simply, Machiavelli was not Machiavellian. His name has come to stand for cynicism and deviousness and ruthlessness and power politics, all because of this little book, *The Prince*. But this is a man who was a profound democrat . . . he wrote not about how he would like things to be like, but how power actually worked, through what he had observed. It's a classic case of shooting the messenger. Here's a man who understood the nature of power and made the mistake of writing it down too clearly." It can be further argued that *The Prince* is a clever way of satirizing the very idea of monarchy by exaggerating its darkest impulses—if power is simply the exploitation of sinister schemes and amoral thinking, then anyone who acquires it is therefore unworthy of respect. It's possible that Machiavelli should be universally beloved—but that's a different argument for a different book. What matters to me is why Machiavelli's connotation will always, always be pejorative, no matter how much unconventional wisdom suggests the opposite. It feels as if it's the central question about his import. So why is this perception unchangeable? What was his mistake?

His mistake was consciousness.

The Prince can be read like a self-help book for someone who openly aspires to be depraved: *This is what's important to believe, this is how the powerful should act in public, this is how you need to behave in private,* et cetera. It's a clinical dissection of how to be tyrannical. Whether Machiavelli believed these things is beside the point—what matters is that he presented them as pure stratagem. It was not an emotional reaction to a specific circumstance; it was a calculated design for life, usable by anyone, applicable anywhere. He turned an autocratic template into entertainment. This is what makes Machiavelli culturally unlikable. It makes him cold. The mere fact that he could *conceive* of these strategies—even if he'd never have used them himself—is what makes him sinister forever. And he is not the only one.

So this, I suspect, is where we *really* begin: In any situation, the villain is the person who knows the most but cares the least.

"Whatever the details of the investigation are, this much is clear to me: There is a villain in this tragedy that lies in that investigation, not in Joe Paterno's response to it."

These are the words of Nike CEO Phil Knight, speaking at Paterno's funeral in January of 2012. The room gave Knight a standing ovation. The world did not.

All funerals are sad, but Paterno's was sad for an uncommon reason. Paterno's funeral was sad because just about everyone who cared about him secretly wished he had died six months earlier. It was sad because it was impossible not to imagine Paterno's final moments, when the only conclusion he could have drawn was that everything he'd done with his life was somehow not worth it. It was sad because the final weeks of his life were far sadder than the literal end of it, and not because of what was happening to his body.

It has always been my belief that people are remembered for the sum of their accomplishments but defined by their singular failure. In the case of Paterno, that supposition does not go far enough. He was, by almost any subjective or objective metric, among the two or three greatest college football coaches of the twentieth century. He finished his career with the most wins in NCAA history, including five undefeated seasons and two national championships. Yet those victories represent only half the equation: For the first forty-five of his forty-six years at Penn State, Paterno was seen as the single-most honorable member in a profession not known for honor. He legitimized collegiate football in the Northeast without jeopardizing the region's academic reputation (a seemingly impossible dream when he took the job in 1966). If you wanted to cite an example of a major college program where the players still went to class, you used Penn State. If you wanted to argue that you could challenge for a national title without bending rules, Penn State was the silver bullet in your rhetorical revolver. This was almost entirely due to one man. Yet all of that will become a secondary memory, solely because Paterno knew something he didn't care about enough.

There's no reason to rehash the details of what happened to Penn State's football program. The story is simple—the team's longtime defensive coordinator, Jerry Sandusky, was a pedophile and a rapist. We'll never know how many adolescent boys he molested during his time at PSU, but he was convicted on forty-five counts. Sandusky was so brazen about his depravity that he forced a ten-year-old boy to have anal sex in the showers of the Nittany Lions' locker room, which is how he was finally caught by a Penn State graduate assistant named Mike McQueary in 2002.

The day after a dumbfounded McQueary witnessed the assault, he went to Paterno and told him what he saw.

This is the point where Paterno ruined his own life.

He did not go to the police, nor did he go to Sandusky and demand that he turn himself in. Instead, he followed the letter of the law: He informed his direct superior, athletic director Tim Curley. Paterno's explanation: "I didn't know what to do. I had not seen anything. Jerry didn't work for me anymore. I didn't have anything to do with him. I tried to look through the Penn State guidelines to see what I was supposed to do. It said I was supposed to call Tim. So I called him." Here is where the unraveling begins. His analysis of the protocol is highly deceptive; referring to Curley as Paterno's "superior" is a little like referring to Rebecca Black as Thom Yorke's "industry peer." Paterno's stature at Penn State dwarfed not only Curley's, but that of the university president. He was more powerful than the totality of the PSU faculty. So even while Paterno followed procedure, he totally failed. He was the only person at Penn State truly accountable for the culture that existed there. He was the only person who could have done anything. And what he chose to do was pretend that this problem did not exist. He coached football for another eight and a half years, until Sandusky was finally busted for sexual impropriety at a high school. The scandal broke and Paterno was terminated. His firing was controversial, because Paterno was deeply beloved (and remains so to all football fans still living in the seventies). Someday, many years from now, the school might rename the Penn State football stadium in this man's honor. It's not outside the realm of possibility. Had Paterno been the actual rapist, he'd still have mild support in central Pennsylvania. But the objective world realized he had to pay. He knew too much and did too little. Two months after his firing, Paterno was dead from lung cancer. Those who interviewed him near the end insisted he wasn't unhappy (in an article for *Sports Illustrated,* Paterno biographer Joe Posnanski reported that a bedridden Paterno was pleased to finally catch up on old episodes of *M*A*S*H,* twenty-nine years after its cancellation). I suppose that's possible, but I'll never believe it. Paterno cared about his reputation at least as much as he cared about winning. This was a guy who majored in English at Brown. His favorite poet was Virgil. He knew how his obit was going to read.

[There's something else here that needs to be mentioned, because it's critical to how the situation is understood: Let's say McQueary doesn't walk into the locker room on that particular day in 2002. Let's say he decides he's hungry and goes to McDonald's instead. He never sees the rape, so he never talks to Paterno. The story still emerges eight years later, and Sandusky still goes to prison. The university is still humiliated. But is Paterno still destroyed? Would he still be at fault? The culture he created at Penn State would still have facilitated the crime. I suppose the question comes down to whether you believe that Paterno *always knew* something was deeply wrong with Sandusky, even before McQueary proved that there was. There had been allegations against Sandusky in 1999, but the initial investigation collapsed. Still, it's hard to accept that Paterno did not suspect there was something askew with his defensive coordinator (particularly since Posnanski's posthumous biography, *Paterno,* claims that JoePa actively disliked Sandusky). Throughout the 1990s, many believed that Sandusky was Paterno's heir apparent as head coach, but he mysteriously retired at the conclusion of the '99 season. Why did he make that decision? Did someone make it for him? We will never know what Paterno knew, but it was certainly more than he admitted. In fact, he might have known *everything.* He even created an exit strategy: During the same month in 2011 that Paterno learned prosecutors were (again) investigating Sandusky, Paterno renegotiated his contract with the university. This new contract would allow him to stop coaching after the 2011 season for a $3 million lump sum, plus the forgiveness of interest-free loans the school had given him totaling $350,000 and use of the university's private plane.]

Sandusky's role in this affair is easy to define: He was the monster. In fact, he was so over-the-top monstrous that people almost stopped thinking about him (according to ESPN media watchdog Patrick Burns, Sandusky's name was mentioned on *SportsCenter* a paltry eight times during the week of Paterno's funeral). McQueary was marginalized as the scenario's coward (evidently because he didn't pull out a crossbow and murder Sandusky in the shower). The children were the helpless victims; the university was the figurehead of institutional evil; the popularity of college football was the atrocity's philosophical root. All those imperfect denouncements are easy. But Paterno's vilification is harder. A handful of media bottom-feeders reveled in his fall, but only to play to the trolls. No normal person wants to hate a dead man he once admired. It feels abnormal and cheap. But what's the alternative? Paterno knew what was happening and chose to intellectually avoid it. He had to choose between humanity and sport, and he picked the one that mattered less. On the day he was finally lowered into the ground, his most adamant defender was the aforementioned Phil Knight, a man who allowed Indonesian children to work in sweatshops so that he could sell $120 basketball shoes to fat American teenagers who didn't play basketball. And then—six months later—even Knight rescinded what he'd said. It was not a good look.

The villain is the person who knows the most but cares the least.

So this is why Machiavelli shall always remain the figure that he is, especially among those who've never questioned why that pejorative connotation exists: He understood the dark. It's not for what he did, because he didn't really do anything; it's for what he understood about other people and for what he understood about himself. He didn't need to commit evil acts. He didn't have to *be* evil. That was just how his mind naturally worked, and that's what discomforts people.

I realize such analysis sounds a little too easy. It seems like I'm suggesting that hardworking dumb people don't like slothful smart people, which ends up seeming like a #HUMBLEBRAG (nobody writes about the intellectual class without latently placing themselves in it, somehow). It also creates a problematic reflection: If a villain is the person who knows the most and cares the least, then a hero is the person who cares too much without knowing anything. It makes every hero seem like Forrest Gump. But it's not the intelligence that people dislike; it's the dispassionate application of that intelligence. It's the *calculation*. It's someone who views life as a game where the rules are poorly written and designed for abuse.

Take George W. Bush: He was an unpopular two-term president. Three times, his approval rating dropped to 25 percent. [To be fair, he also had the highest approval rating of all time, very briefly. But that was immediately after 9/11—and in the wake of domestic terrorism, a well-dressed mannequin's approval rating might have hovered around 50.] During his last two years in office, he was hammered nonstop, periodically classified as the worst U.S. president since Ulysses Grant or James Buchanan. Yet was Bush a villain? No. He was not. He was never, ever calculating. He didn't know the most (which is not to say he was dumb), and he didn't care the least (which is not to say he was a paragon of empathy). He was just the guy who ended up with the job. The villain of his administration ended up being Vice President Dick Cheney, a frosty puppet master who radically expanded the powers of the presidency even though he was not the president. He didn't seem to care about anyone, including himself.

Republicans are doggedly vilified within the media's hipper sectors, but not always in predictable ways (and certainly not for their *level* of malevolence, which seems almost arbitrary). Malleable, forgettable Mitt Romney was the GOP's presidential nominee in 2012, but he was vilified only by the type of ideologue intent on vilifying whoever fell into that role. [It was more sporting to obsessively dislike his running mate, the precocious yet middle-aged Paul Ryan. Ryan admitted that he used to read novelist Ayn Rand, a compulsion now perceived as considerably worse than classifying John Wilkes Booth as an underrated stage actor.] During the race for the Republican nomination, it initially appeared that Texas governor Rick Perry was destined to wear the villain's cowl. It was almost too easy: Perry consciously embodied the caricature liberals had always wanted G. W. Bush to be. But even Bush saw Perry as distasteful. This was a man who took personal pride in state executions (during a televised debate, he stated that he'd "never struggled" with the possibility that even one of the 234 prisoners he'd killed during his governorship might have been innocent). Perry wanted to be the villain, probably for strategic reasons. But it didn't take. He wasn't smart enough; he probably didn't even know how "Ayn" was pronounced. The low point was when Perry confidently insisted he would immediately eliminate three governmental agencies upon election, yet could not remember what those agencies were. Perry didn't scare anyone; sure, he might sentence you to lethal injection, but he also might confuse the potassium chloride with Diet Dr Pepper. He was a man without a plan. This is why the 2012 Republican villain became Newt Gingrich, a man with more plans than any human on earth. Gingrich wanted to eliminate child labor laws, which would have seemed extreme had he not also wanted to colonize the moon. For a while, he held all his media press conferences inside zoos (before addressing the NRA, he was bitten by a penguin). He had so many crazy, interesting, quasi-diabolical plans that there was simply no way he could be president. Even when he surged in the polls, he never had a chance; you can't be that clever and that devoid of compassion without engendering more hate than affection. (Once, when asked to describe himself in one word, Gingrich said, "Cheerful," which was the cognitive equivalent of "Go fuck yourself for asking that question.") Even when his most loyal supporters discussed his candidacy, they felt obligated to preface their use of the word "genius" with modifiers like "unpredictable" and "perverse." And that did not bother him; Gingrich loves who he is. He doesn't care what other people think of him, because he doesn't particularly care about other people. This is charming, problematic, and extraordinarily effective—particularly as a means of appealing to committed anti-ideologues who spend their lives worrying about the problem of false authenticity. "I've had the great pleasure of meeting Newt Gingrich and having a chat with the fellow on a staircase," ex–Sex Pistols vocalist John Lydon once told *Rolling Stone.* "I found him completely dishonest and totally likable, because he doesn't care." This is both the highest compliment a Sex Pistol can dispense and an incisive description of Newt's character. He *exclusively* cares about ideas, regardless of their merits. He would tie a woman to the railroad tracks just to prove he knew what time the train left the station. This is why I always find myself rooting for him, even when I'm against what he purports to desire. I know exactly what he's doing. It's like looking into a mirror I do not possess the capacity to smash.

ANOTHER THING
THAT INTERESTS ME ABOUT
THE EAGLES IS THAT I
[AM CONTRACTUALLY OBLIGATED TO]
HATE THEM

Here are the opening lyrics to the song "Take It Easy" by the Eagles. It was the first cut on the Eagles' first album; written by Glenn Frey and Jackson Browne, "Take It Easy" was released upon the world in May of 1972, one month before I was born. The words are familiar to anyone who listens to rock on the radio, a population that dwindles with every passing year . . .

> Well, I'm running down the road
> Tryin' to loosen my load
> I've got seven women on my mind
> Four that wanna own me
> Two that wanna stone me
> One says she's a friend of mine

I'd love to isolate the first time I heard these words, but I can't. It predates my memory. I do, however, remember the first time I *thought* about these words, which didn't happen until 2003. I was intrigued by the math: The main character (who's technically the creation of non-Eagle Browne, since he wrote this particular verse) is fleeing from seven women. Four of these females are possessive, so he finds them unappealing; two others hate him (but don't want to own him), which comes across as neutral; the seventh is (I think) the one he likes, but she can't reciprocate. It's clearly the problem of a young man, as no one over thirty-five could sustain interest in seven simultaneous relationships unless they're biracial and amazing at golf. The four who want to own him are sympathetic; the two who want to stone him are reasonable; the one who says she's his friend is the O. Henry twist. Now, are we supposed to *like* this philandering protagonist? Not necessarily, although I suspect we're supposed to see him as a realist who's slowly realizing he's made his own life more complex than necessary. If we allow ourselves to project the unknown motives of the songwriter even further, perhaps we start to think the song is about the discomfort of romantic honesty; maybe we start to think the verse is really about how each of these seven women has reacted to the abrupt awareness of the other six (four increase their affection, two invert their affection, and one slips into detachment). If you conject even further, perhaps you can pretend the song is only about one woman (with seven different sides to her personality), or that this is supposed to be humor, or that we're not supposed to think about these seven women as actual people, or that we're not supposed to think about these lyrics at all.

However, one detail is non-negotiable: People fucking hate this song.

Which is not to say it's unpopular or unpleasant or a failure, because those descriptions don't apply. It went to number twelve on the Billboard charts, and only an idiot would argue that "Take It Easy" is poorly written or badly executed. When it originally hit the radio, some guy from *Rolling Stone* claimed it was the best-sounding song of 1972. If we use all of America as an aesthetic gauge (and particularly its Walmarts, gas stations, and retail yarn proprietors), this song is a classic. But pop music—like all subcultures—has an outside culture and an inside culture. Pop music's exterior culture is why the Eagles are the best-selling rock band in U.S. history; its interior culture reviles the Eagles so much that almost nothing written about them can ignore that reality. Barney Hoskins's 2005 book about the Laurel Canyon scene that spawned the band takes its title from the group's biggest hit ("Hotel California") but still can't ignore how they were perceived by their peers: "For Gram Parsons, the success of the radio-friendly Eagles was galling." *To the Limit,* a sympathetic (almost sycophantic) 1998 biography of the group, tries to spin their bad reviews into understated masculinity: "We'd been abused by the press, so we developed a 'fuck you' attitude toward them," says drummer/vocalist Don Henley. These are established positions, understood by everyone who cares. It's not like I'm exposing some dark secret or pushing a false controversy: The musical reputation of the Eagles is great and the social reputation of the Eagles is terrible. They are the most unpopular super-popular entity ever created by California, not counting Ronald Reagan.

I know this because everybody knows this, but also because—once—I hated the Eagles, too. After spending the first twenty-five years of my life believing they were merely boring, I suddenly decided they were the worst band that had ever existed (or could ever exist). I'd unconsciously internalized all the complaints that supposedly made them despicable: They were rich hippies. They were virtuosos in an idiom that did not require virtuosity. They were self-absorbed Hollywood liberals. They were not-so-secretly shallow. They were uncaring womanizers and the worst kind of cokeheads. They wanted to be seen as cowboys, but not the ones who actually rode horses. They *never* rocked, even after adding Joe Walsh for that express purpose (the first forty-five seconds of "Life in the Fast Lane" are a push). They lectured college kids about their environmental footprint while flying around in private jets. They literally called themselves "The Eagles." It was easy to hate a band who kept telling me to take it easy when I was quite obviously trying to do so already.

And then, one day in 2003, I stopped hating them.

This is not because of anything they did or anything I did. It wasn't due to anything except clarity. I was working at a magazine, and Warner Bros. mailed me a promotional copy of *The Very Best of the Eagles*. I slid the CD into the disk drive of my computer and waited for the music to start. Once again, the first track was "Take It Easy." It sounded okay, but—then again—it had always *sounded* okay. I'd accidentally heard this song hundreds of times in my life, so there wasn't going to be any big surprise. It was the same song it had always been, remastered but unchanged. The only thing that was different was how I felt about the band itself: Suddenly, I felt nothing. I did not hate them. I didn't *love* them, but I certainly didn't view their subsistence as problematic or false or socially sinister. They were just an old rock band who made music that was significant and relaxing and inevitable, and who seemed to be hated (particularly by people like myself) for reasons that were both valid and ridiculous. So I listened to "Take It Easy" and I thought about its lyrical content, and I came to a mostly positive—but highly uncomfortable—realization about who I was and how I thought about art.

I no longer possessed the capacity to hate rock bands.

I started caring about pop music as a fifth grader, but it didn't make me lose my grip on reality until the summer before seventh grade. That was 1984. For the next twenty years, I didn't care about anything else with as much unbridled intensity, except for women and amateur athletics and booze and (of course) all the self-made problems that accompany those specific pursuits. Because I loved music so much, I hated it even more—but my reasons for disliking music were never as valid as my reasons for enjoying it. What follows is a chronology of every artist I most despised from age twelve to age thirty-one, followed by a brief analysis of what I did not like about them at the time . . .

1984 (**Bruce Springsteen**): There's never been an artist I didn't like as much as I didn't like Bruce Springsteen as a twelve-year-old. I hated all his songs, including the ones I'd never heard of. I hated music about roads and I hated his generic-yet-kinetic clothing and I hated whoever it was I thought he represented, which I imagined to be humorless people who wanted to vote for Gary Hart. I just thought he was so *fake,* which is the most backward possible reason for hating Bruce Springsteen. But—for me, at the time, having no idea who Holden Caulfield even was—my definition of fakeness was fanatically nuanced. I made extremely subtle distinctions. My favorite band was Mötley Crüe, whom I also viewed as fake—but the difference was that Mötley Crüe did not *pretend* they were real (or at least not in a convincing enough manner). Vince Neil never led me to believe that any element about who he pretended to be was supposed to serve any purpose beyond "the act of being the singer in Mötley Crüe." Yet old people who read *Newsweek* believed Bruce was somehow different from everyone else making music, and his willingness to perpetuate that fallacy made me view his integrity as profoundly compromised. It seemed like the difference between acting in a play and lying in real life. [Obviously, time has passed and my feelings have changed. I now view Springsteen as an upright citizen who's recorded more good songs than the vast majority of people who have ever tried to do so. I am his fan, sort of. But not completely. Any time I meet someone who thinks Springsteen is overrated or artificial, I find myself thinking, "This person is extra real." I immediately respect that person more. And yet I *do* sincerely believe Springsteen is (on balance) a great guy. I don't hate him at all. So why am I still retroactively trolling him? It's just something I can't get over.]

1985 (Bruce Springsteen): This was an emotional hangover from 1984. I was a grammar school red giant collapsing into a middle school white dwarf; my anti-Boss feelings grew dense and intense (super hot and extra useless). Why did he use the word *speedball* instead of *fastball* when reminiscing about high school sports? Was he trying to sound dumb on purpose? Was ESPN unavailable in New Jersey? An episode of *Growing Pains* was built around on Mike Seaver (Kirk Cameron) wanting to see Springsteen in concert—and so did his fictional father (Alan Thicke). I suppose Springsteen was the first major artist for which this commonality was plausible: If someone had youngish parents, it was theoretically possible for a fifteen-year-old kid to love the same singer as his father. I found this kinship alien and undesirable, although now it probably happens all the time (in certain Brooklyn neighborhoods, it's actually an ordinance). That said, I don't remember Bruce being popular with *any* of the kids at my school, even casually. The teachers seemed to like him more than the students. He used to be so much older then; he's younger than that now. Springsteen used to be the same age as Steve Winwood, but now he's maybe six years older than Julian Casablancas.

1986 (Van Halen): This temporary distaste for VH was solely a product of my inflexible (almost fascist) support of David Lee Roth's solo career and my dislike of anyone who thought *5150* was better than *1984* (an opinion I deemed "unserious"). Hating Van Halen required an astronomical degree of nerfherdian gymnastics, particularly since Roth essentially destroyed a band I loved and then tried to act like he'd been unjustly fired. But I've always been like this; when Mötley Crüe split up in 1991, I sided with Vince. Within any group conflict, my loyalties inevitably rest with whichever person is most obviously wrong. I feel like I started appreciating *5150* around the same time Randy Moss started playing for the Minnesota Vikings, but I don't think those two things have any relationship outside of my personal memory and the content of this specific sentence.

1987 (**Dire Straits**): My reasoning here is not particularly reasonable. Basically, I (and everyone I trusted, which was maybe five other people in the entire world) misinterpreted the lyrics to the song "Money for Nothing," which had actually been on the radio for two years before I got around to hating it. We all thought that when Mark Knopfler sang, *"That little faggot with the earring and the makeup / Yeah, buddy, that's his own hair,"* he was criticizing glam bands like Cinderella and Faster Pussycat. [I now realize those lyrics were actually mimicking some random bozo who worked inside a kitchen appliance store and liked to spew opinions about MTV during his cigarette break. But these kinds of things were impossible to know in 1987.] I decided Mark Knopfler was a soft, anti-metal hypocrite, which makes only slightly less sense than believing Springsteen was a fraudulent poseur. Weirdly, I was not remotely troubled by the song's language; being a high school sophomore, it had not yet occurred to me that the word *faggot* could be viewed as offensive to anyone who wasn't literally gay. I stopped hating Dire Straits around the same time I started defending H. Ross Perot, but neither entity truly migrated into my mental universe. The fact that I insist on always referring to Mark Knopfler as "Mark Knopfler" is probably proof: our relationship remains formal. I dig "Sultans of Swing," but if someone said, "Hey Chuck—Warner Brothers has just released a DVD with some amazing footage from the *Brothers in Arms* tour," I would probably avoid watching it by pretending I'd already seen it.

1988 (**R.E.M.**): I didn't relate to the kind of person who related to R.E.M. and I didn't like textured, nonheavy songs that made me feel like some dour weirdo was telling me I was living my life wrong. Over the next twenty years, R.E.M. would become one of my favorite bands of all time, which means a) the sixteen-year-old version of me would have hated the thirty-six-year-old version of me, and b) I probably *was* living my life wrong.

1989 (**Fine Young Cannibals**): Though I could not name one member of the group or one fact about their history, I didn't like them as people (and was annoyed that "She Drives Me Crazy" was so obviously not terrible). Their fan base had progressive haircuts and trendy clothes, qualities I considered unpatriotic. Everything turned around when I found out they selected their band name by randomly opening *Leonard Maltin's Movie Guide*. Now I think they're a bunch of geniuses.

1990 (**R.E.M.**): The use of "Stand" in the opening credits of *Get a Life* galvanized my fear that I was losing an undeclared war against reality. How could Chris Elliott support this? I decided to stop rooting for the Georgia Bulldogs.

1991 (**The Red Hot Chili Peppers**): They seemed like all the idiots at my college who were constantly starting terrible bands and failing organic chemistry, except these idiots were famous and never wore shirts.

1992 (**The Red Hot Chili Peppers**): In the video for the proto-pussy smack ballad "Under the Bridge," Anthony Kiedis runs along the Los Angeles River in slow motion. His arms cross his body; he had terrible running form. I also recall adamantly disagreeing with the assertion that Flea's bass playing was (in any way) comparable to that of Les Claypool from Primus. My 1992 concerns were oblique. I purchased a kerosene lamp in order to impress strangers who wandered into my dorm room in order to tell me I was playing Primus too loud. It was the style of the time.

1993 (Mr. Bungle): I knew an interesting person who believed this self-indulgent side project was way more interesting than it actually was, thereby serving as my real-world introduction to The Problem of Overrated Ideas. The group's singer was improvisational and gross, musically and otherwise. He once told a story on *MTV News* about how—for his own amusement—he used to eat huge portions of instant mashed potatoes, chased with an entire bottle of schnapps. He would then stroll into a local laundromat, open washers and dryers at random, and vomit onto strangers' clothes. I could not identify with this behavior, although I don't suppose that was his intention. Couldn't he have just taken the L7 route and chucked bloody tampons at teenagers? At least that sustained the cycle of life. I found greater comfort with the singer's other band, a more "conventionally alternative" collective with a spattering of mainstream popularity and some unanticipated insights into smoking angel dust and competitive pumpkin farming.

1994 (Pink Floyd): I was driving through suburban Minneapolis at dusk when something off *The Wall* came on the radio, prompting me to conclude that I was being intellectually crucified by an army of forty-year-old library patrons who couldn't accept that cannabis was still illegal. I could never feel this way now, except in unconditional reverse. But I was twenty-two, an age where the commercial past always seems to be wrecking the limitless future; I was open- and close-minded at the same time. The Moody Blues were another band I hated that summer—they seemed like dead people I was supposed to learn about on PBS. Oh well. We all eventually become whatever we pretend to hate.

1995 (Ted Nugent): This one is tricky. I'm not sure if I decided to hate Ted Nugent because I was really into Tori Amos (which I was) or if I was just trying to sleep with a woman who worked at a candle shop and was really, *really* into Tori Amos (mixed results on this strategy). Maybe I just thought Ted was childish and uncool, qualities I intermittently worried about when not listening to KISS records. This aforementioned candle clerk came over to my apartment on Halloween and we played *Double Live Gonzo*, just to make condescending comments about its vagina-obsessed lyrics and retrograde aesthetic (although I still wonder why she wasn't more skeptical of the fact that I owned four albums by an artist I supposedly hated). Further complicating matters was my parallel obsession with the Replacements' *Let It Be*, which suggested (at least on "Gary's Got a Boner") that Bob Stinson thought the Nuge was a sonic mastermind who should have been elected governor of Michigan.

1996 **(Blur):** The Oasis vs. Blur feud had actually transpired the year before, but I was living in pre-Internet North Dakota and received my culture news roughly nine months after the fact (which was preferable, though I did not know this at the time). The notion of Blur pretending it had a "rivalry" with Oasis still strikes me as comically obscene; it would be no different than RC Cola trying to start a war with Coke. But my larger issue was a perceived differential in class: Every time I met someone who thought Blur was better than Oasis, it inevitably meant they thought like a rich person (so either they *were* rich, or they were raised with upper-middle-class sensibilities in a lower-class world). Blur was Britpop for American kids who wore neckties on campus and turtlenecks to keg parties; it was Britpop for American kids who could actually afford to spend a semester in Britain. I'll concede that Blur has a handful of better than decent songs—I'd estimate around nine, plus the semi-ironic one that always gets blasted at hockey games—but it's hard to imagine a snootier collective. Equally troubling was Damon Albarn's well-publicized sex life with the striking lead singer from Elastica, an accomplishment that made me suspect he was taunting the proletariat with his semen.

1997 (**Phish**): 'Twas the apex of my deeply unoriginal I-hate-hippies phase, which some people do not grow out of. Of course, I was also into Bob Marley and Jimi Hendrix (and Ben Harper!) at the time, so what the fuck did I know about hippies? Did I not realize hippies could be black?

1998 (**The Eagles**): Here was a turning point. Many things were happening simultaneously. One was that I had started to erroneously believe subjective criticism was more important than objective reporting; another was that I saw *The Big Lebowski* and decided the main character should become the model for all human thought. Electronica was on MTV, so music videos were mostly just Asian teenagers playing Ping-Pong and time-elapse photography of melting plastic cubes. *Seinfeld* was going off the air, so even grandmas were temporary postmodernists. Aspirant Urban Outfitter employees were excited about technology and really into Neutral Milk Hotel. It was the logical time to believe Glenn Frey was Pol Pot.

1999 (**The Eagles**): *The Big Lebowski* became available on VHS.

2000 (**U2**): I borrowed the documentary *Rattle and Hum* from the Akron Public Library, which would have been fine if I hadn't subsequently watched it. I can only assume this movie makes U2 hate U2: The band is so consumed with their sincere adoration of southern black culture that they somehow seem marginally racist.

2001 (**Coldplay**): I wrote a book in 2001 where I claim, "Coldplay is the shittiest fucking band I've ever heard in my entire fucking life." This is possibly the most memorable thing I've ever written, and arguably the stupidest. My intention (at the time) was to illustrate how people use popular culture to explain their own lives to themselves, and that I was hating Coldplay in order to avoid hating myself. But (of course) almost no one who purchased this book made that inference, which (of course) is nobody's fault but mine. I still meet teenagers who attempt to ingratiate themselves by telling me how much they hate Coldplay. And while I *did* hate the tenor of their music (and still can't bear listening to it, even when I'm shopping for trousers), I regret being so profane. It was cheap. It feels like I threw a rock at Gwyneth Paltrow's gazebo.

2002 **(Blur):** I'd just moved to New York and discovered that people were still arguing about this, except Oasis was now a 7½-point underdog. Even poor people in New York think like rich people.

2003 **(Yeah Yeah Yeahs):** Nobody seemed willing to admit that this band (and particularly the guitarist) were postpunk joker zombies who sang power ballads about cartography. I don't enjoy music that sounds broken on purpose; that's supposed to happen by accident. In later years, I would grow to appreciate the singer's solo attempt at "Immigrant Song" during the opening credits of that fourteen-hour movie about the Swedish tattoo artist who murders somebody with a Xerox machine, but the YYYs will always be fake art. They put way too much effort into acting like they were pretending to work hard at casual brilliance. Now that I think about it, they are the opposite of the Eagles.

There are fifteen artists on this list. Seven are already in the (admittedly meaningless) Rock and Roll Hall of Fame, and two others will get there eventually. Twelve of them have recorded at least one song I love. They've all been hugely or marginally successful, except for maybe Mr. Bungle. But I hated them all, at least provisionally. And it wasn't just that I didn't like hearing the music or seeing their faces on MTV—it had something to do with viewing them as representations of what I wanted to be against. I didn't see the artists I loved as heroic, but I saw the artists I hated as villainous. And that is a feeling I can no longer feel. Somewhere in 2003, my ability to hate the Eagles (or Coldplay, or Dave Matthews, or Mumford and Sons, or whoever) just evaporated. I could no longer construct antipathy for random musicians, even if they deserved it. My personality had calcified and emancipated itself from taste. I still cared about music, but not enough to feel emotionally distraught over its nonmusical expansion into celebrity and society. And this was a real problem. Being emotionally fragile is an important part of being a successful critic; it's an integral element to being engaged with mainstream art, assuming you aspire to write about it in public. If you hate everything, you're a banal asshole . . . but if you don't hate *anything,* you're boring. You're useless. And you end up writing about why you can no longer generate fake feelings that other people digest as real.

There needs to be more awareness about the cultural impact of reverse engineering, particularly as it applies to fandom and revulsion. It's the most important part of describing the day-to-day import of art, which is ultimately what criticism is supposed to do. But there are no critics who can admit to their own reverse engineering without seeming underinformed. It's like arguing that the greatest Russian novel ever written happens to be the only one you ever finished.

Still, there are examples of this everywhere.

Take someone like Taylor Swift, a one-woman "Hotel California": When Swift's second album came out (2008's *Fearless*), she was a regionally famous Nashville artist that most casual pop fans had never thought much about. But *Fearless* crossed over, and she was suddenly being noticed by people who traditionally ignored mainstream country. Because her songs were excellent (and because any genre slightly different from rock feels initially fresh to rockist ears), everyone decided that *Fearless* was great—and not only great, but culturally important. Mere appreciation of the music was not enough. This necessitated the unconscious construction of a reality where Swift herself could be taken seriously. So how could this be accomplished? The first step was to always mention her age as proof of unprecedented maturity: She was sixteen when she released her first album and eighteen for *Fearless*, but she seemed to handle her notoriety with unusual deftness and professionalism (Kanye West stormed onstage while she was accepting a trophy at the MTV Music Awards, but Swift's response was measured and polite). She was an adult woman inside a teenage girl, and that validated the highbrow appreciation of a song like "You Belong with Me." (Her fictional depictions of teen anguish were consumed as suburban realness.) The quality of her songs caused people to value her as a concept. But this worked too well. Swift became so abstractly imperative that she turned into a celebrity in the *US Weekly* sense: She became famous to people who'd never heard her music. All the qualities her previous audience had once used to justify her success as a pop star felt annoying to those who were caring about her for the first time. To the casual observer, she seemed unconvincingly shocked by her own success and obsessed with her market share. Instead of coming across as mature, it scanned as calculating. And this preexisting assumption is what new audiences injected into her third album, 2010's *Speak Now*. The record was massive, but Swift got hammered for her self-absorption and a propensity for nostalgic oversharing (two qualities singer-songwriters are *supposed* to possess—but not, apparently, the young female ones). When she wrote about a failed relationship with John Mayer ("Dear John"), it seemed fake and exploitive, even though the love affair had actually happened. When she made a video for a song about the cruelty of critics ("Mean"), she literally tied herself to the railroad tracks and tried to convince capricious fans that she still self-identified as a marginalized victim. But that only worked on people who had never questioned her pose to begin with.

Now, the easy explanation for this shift in perception is "backlash." But that's only how it looks from the outside. What really happened is this: People who liked Taylor Swift's music reverse-engineered a scenario in which they could appreciate her for non-musical reasons; two years later, different people who loathed that construction had to find a way to preexplain why they weren't going to enjoy her material (so they infused their prefab distaste of her persona back into her work). When Swift cowrote "We Are Never Ever Getting Back Together" with Swedish hit machine Max Martin, critics could not deny that it was catchy and practical, so now they had to pretend it was an empowering takedown of Donnie Darko. [The reason behind everything always has to be something else entirely.]

How this principle applies to the Eagles is straightforward: They seemed like counterculture figures who were against the values of the counterculture (and it's always the counterculture who gets to decide the long-term likability of any rock artist). They aspired to (and achieved) commercial hugeness; nothing about their magnitude was accidental. Soft-spoken replacement bassist Timothy B. Schmit was the only Eagle born in the state of California, yet they effortlessly represented what people do not like about Malibu. They were the antithesis of *The Rockford Files*. While many of their arena-rock peers were misogynist for how they physically interacted with groupies, the Eagles directed their distaste toward the secret interior motives all hot women allegedly possessed ("Witchy Woman" being the easiest example, "Lyin' Eyes" being the most direct). Basically, they just seemed mean-spirited and wealthy. They were annoying to the type of person who is susceptible to annoyance. Which is how many people (including myself) choose to hear their songs. What do you make of a band that writes a disco track about how disco is insidious? I still don't know. I know what words I'm supposed to throw around—"cynical," "self-reflexive," "clinical"—but I wonder if I'd use those words if I didn't know Don Henley was the man who'd written the song. I fear I'm just describing *him* with those words, even though *I do hear those qualities* when I listen to "The Disco Strangler."

But here's what changed, inside my skull: Those qualities no longer make me hate Henley or his band. Instead, they make me appreciate the song itself with a complexity I cannot pretend to understand. They make me realize that I cannot be trusted about anything, and that I can't even trust myself.

I appreciate "The Disco Strangler" because I now realize (and cannot *unrealize*) that this entire process is a closed circuit, happening inside my false consciousness. The only outside element is the sound wave containing the sonic signature—everything about its latent meaning and its larger merit is being imagined and manipulated by my brain's unwillingness to hold an unexplained opinion. If I like a song (or if I dislike a song), I have to explain—to myself—why that feeling exists. If I'm writing about the song in a public forum, I have to explain it to other people. But my explanation is never accurate unless I flatly declare, "I like this and I don't know why" or "I dislike this for reasons that can't be quantified." Every other response is the process of taking an abstract feeling and figuring out how I can fit it into a lexicon that matches whatever I already want to believe. My mind is not my own. And once that realization calcifies internally, there is no going back. Once you realize you can't control how you feel, it's impossible to believe any of your own opinions. As a result, I can't hate the Eagles. It feels impossible. It feels stupid. The Eagles are real, but they don't exist; they only exist as a way to think about "the Eagles."

So often does it happen that we live our lives in chains, and we never even know there is no key.

VILLAINS

WHO ARE NOT VILLAINS

Here's a list of anonymous people who—in theory—are bad citizens and social pariahs:

1) Men who hijack airplanes.
2) Con artists.
3) Funk narcissists.
4) Drug dealers.
5) Athletes who use race as a means for taunting an opponent.

Here is a list of charismatic people who—under specific circumstances, and when injected with a high dose of false emotional attachment—can never be villains:

1) Men who hijack airplanes.
2) Con artists.
3) Funk narcissists.
4) Drug dealers.
5) Athletes who use race as a means for taunting an opponent.

In 1977, Keith Richards was arrested for heroin possession in Canada. It was his fourth drug-related arrest within a span of ten years. It looked like he might go to prison for real. However, his ultimate sentence was not exactly Alcatraz: He was asked to perform a benefit concert for the blind before flying to Paris and recording *Some Girls*. "Usually the guy in the black hat gets killed in the end," Richards said when questioned about this incident thirty-five years later. "But not this time. Not this time."

Not this time.

And if your name happens to be Keith Richards, "this time" translates as "ever."

Unreality abhors consistency.

A man boards an airplane in Portland, headed to Seattle on a thirty-minute afternoon flight. It's the day before Thanksgiving. The man wears a dark suit and a black tie; he orders a highball from the flight attendant. Over time, these choices will define almost everything about his character.

The plane separates from Earth. The man in the suit slips a note to a stewardess, but she jams it into her pocket, unread. She assumes it's a romantic advance, because all of this is happening in 1971 (an era when female flight attendants were hired for their looks and assumed to be promiscuous). A few minutes later, the man pulls her aside. "You better read that note," he says. "I have a bomb."

The confession is shocking, but not surprising: Throughout the 1960s, political dissidents hijacked commercial airlines with surprising regularity, usually followed by a demand to be flown to Cuba. In 1970, Palestinian radicals managed to hijack three planes simultaneously, diverting all three to Jordan. There was still a robust hijacking culture. But this man's note is unique. His demands are not political. They are simple and specific: Land the plane. Remove all passengers, but keep the crew intact. Get me $200,000 in nonsequential twenties. Bring me four parachutes (two standard backpacks and two emergency chestpacks). "No funny business," the note concludes. The man shows the flight attendant the inside of a briefcase, which (indeed) houses a bomb (or at least a bomblike facsimile). The man in the suit remains polite. "A gentleman," insists Tina Mucklow, the Northwest Orient stewardess who spends the most time with him. "He seemed rather nice . . . thoughtful and calm." Subsequent police sketches will make this man look like a hungover Bing Crosby, but the best modifier for his appearance will always be "nondescript": Caucasian, six feet tall, 175 pounds, brown eyes, brown hair, no whiskers. He chain-smokes cigarettes and seems to know a lot about commercial airplanes (how long they take to fuel, how fast they need to travel to maintain a specific altitude, the mechanics of the plane's rarely used aft staircase, et cetera). The plane finally lands in Sea-Tac Airport. The money and the parachutes are delivered on time. His plan is working. He releases the other passengers, most of whom have no idea that a hijacking has even occurred. An official with the FAA advises the man to surrender and informs him that the maximum penalty for air piracy is death. The man in the suit is unimpressed.

The Boeing 727 is refueled. The man in the suit, one stewardess (Mucklow), and the flight crew return to the air, theoretically headed to Mexico via Reno. It's a long flight, so they will need to take on more fuel in Nevada. When the 727 reaches the low cruising altitude of ten thousand feet (as specified by the hijacker's note), the man in the dark suit tells Mucklow to join the pilots in the cockpit and lock the door. By now, night has descended on the Pacific Northwest. Sleet pelts the aircraft. Around 8 P.M., a red light illuminates on the jet's instrument panel, indicating that the door to the aft staircase is ajar. Through the intercom, the pilot asks the man, "Is there anything we can do for you?" His response is monosyllabic: "No." Two hours later, the 727 lands in Reno; after a wordless five-minute pause, they finally open the door to the cabin. The man is gone, and so is the cash (although, oddly, he's left behind his clip-on tie). By process of elimination, the FBI deduces the man's identity from the flight manifest: Dan Cooper. A Portland reporter erroneously identifies the suspect as "D. B. Cooper," and—for a variety of innocuous reasons—the incorrect name sticks. And it sticks forever, because the man in the suit is never found.

D. B. Cooper hijacked a plane with a bomb for money, and he probably failed. But he is not a villain. He's a folk hero, and that doesn't even feel weird.

The man had confidence.

Who can hate the confidence man? Only those who know him. Read a book like David Maurer's 1940 nonfiction classic *The Big Con* and try to view con men as inherently evil people—it's impossible. Maurer's blow-by-blow description of every criminal act only serves to increase their appeal. "Confidence men are not *crooks* in the ordinary sense of the word," the author states in the book's third paragraph. "They are suave, slick, and capable. Their depredations are very much on the genteel side." A few sentences later, Maurer defines the con artist's saving grace: "The confidence man prospers only because of the fundamental dishonesty of his victims." It's assumed that whoever the con man swindles is partially at fault, because you can't con an honest man (a "long con" can only succeed if the mark is actively implicated in the crime, because that's what stops him from going to the police). Over time, this judgment became the vortex of the con-man archetype. We like to view confidence men as street-smart scalawags who prey on all the frauds who aren't as smart as they pretend. They're technically part of the underworld, but they're more associated with the underclass.

This is especially true in situations that aren't real.

David Mamet (America's greatest con-obsessed screenwriter) has made two films in which confidence men are heartless villains: 1987's *House of Games* and 1997's *The Spanish Prisoner*. In both movies, the con men are exceedingly charming until it's too late, mirroring the actual experience of being bamboozled. But this type of narrative is rare. In most con-artist stories—*The Sting, Paper Moon, The Grifters, Matchstick Men, Catch Me if You Can, White*

Men Can't Jump, and even *The Music Man*—every unearthed detail about who the con man is makes us more empathetic toward his vocation. Usually, he (or she) has complex feelings about taking money from strangers. Often, he's been socially crippled by some kind of past emotional trauma, usually involving his parents. If a film involves multiple confidence men, the con artist we "know" the most is inevitably double-crossed by his (inevitably less ethical and less explained) partner. He's never as immoral as the person he works with. There's always this underlying message that—if we could only *understand* the inner con man—we would love him. But this is not something that's true; it's only something we believe.

Once, while drinking in a bar in Washington, D.C., I expressed philosophical admiration for con men to an acquaintance of mine (at the time, I was actually reading *The Big Con*). I mentioned how much I like movies about confidence men, and I casually wondered if grifting people would be something I'd excel at. My acquaintance looked at me like I'd just vomited on his baby. "But don't you find con men fascinating?" I asked him directly. He proceeded to tell me about his father, a man who made a bad living by pretending to be a minister at multiple churches in order to embezzle money from widows within the various congregations. When that scheme finally collapsed, he quietly used his teenage son's Social Security number to obtain illegal credit cards, which he never paid back (for the next ten years, my acquaintance was burdened with a massive debt and an obliterated credit rating). His father ruined the lives of everyone in his family, and then he disappeared.

"So . . . no," my friend finally said. "I do not find con men fascinating."

I felt guilty for what I'd said moments earlier. I felt childish. I apologized. But I also silently wondered: If my acquaintance's life was a made-for-TV movie, who would be my favorite character in the script? And why is that so different from the story I just heard?

* * *

The 1984 movie *Purple Rain* is unforgettable for many reasons: the live performance of "Darling Nikki," its underrated examination of what constitutes art, the unexpected cameo from Apollonia's breasts, and the discomfiting nostalgia it evokes for that bygone era when Prince seemed way weirder than Michael Jackson. The film has a lot to offer, except for acting. But its single most memorable element will always be the inclusion of Morris Day, an antagonist so self-assured that he ends up being twice as endearing as the hero he antagonizes.

The premise of *Purple Rain* is rote. We have a struggling Minneapolis-based musician known as "The Kid" (Prince) who longs for success, but everyone (at least in his mind) is against him. Unlike most rock films, his problems are not an extension of drugs or booze or poverty. His dilemmas are purely artistic: His abusive father doesn't respect his musical ability. Local club owners are disturbed by his indulgent, uncompromising pop art ("Nobody digs your music but yourself," the owner of First Avenue tells him directly, a sentiment shared by everyone living inside Prince's imagination). His own band views him as paranoid and controlling. Even his love life is a musical concern—the reason the loss of his girlfriend is so painful is that she becomes enamored with The Kid's professional rival. That rival is Morris Day. In *Purple Rain*, Day plays an amplified version of himself. He is the frontman for a group called The Time, which (in reality) was created by Prince in 1981, an extension of Prince's contract with Warner Bros. that allowed him to develop other artists. When Morris Day and The Time toured with Prince and the Revolution in 1982, a real rivalry between the two bands emerged; this professional animosity was the catalyst for the film's musical conflict. As fictionalized in *Purple Rain*, we're supposed to feel sympathy for Prince and antipathy toward Day. In theory, this makes sense: Morris Day presents himself as an egocentric pimp who demeans his subordinates, mocks suicide, tosses women into garbage Dumpsters, and requires his onstage sidekick (the sycophantic Jerome) to literally hold up a mirror during concerts so that Morris can admire his own reflection. This fake version of Morris Day is a progenitor of the real Chris Brown, the self-absorbed R&B superstar who assaulted Rihanna in 2009 and was instantly despised by everyone in America (except Rihanna herself, who seemed to like him slightly more). Morris Day should be easy to hate. But that's not what happens.

What happens is that you root for Prince to succeed, but only out of obligation. This is a movie and you're the audience, and you understand what movie audiences are supposed to do. In the same way that Prince fashions an on-screen character after himself, we fashion ourselves as people who pull for the film's hero and feel satisfied when he overcomes adversity. We accept our emotional responsibilities and adhere to film grammar, at least during the 111 minutes we're occupied with the story. We are against Morris Day, because the narrative derails if we support him. But once the credits roll and the picture ends, Morris instantly becomes more likable than Prince, even though Day's behavior was (technically) more boorish. Morris steals the movie and remains its greatest creation. He exists as a charming goofball who's more "real" than Prince, despite being fabricated in every way (except for his name).

So why does this happen?

It happens because Day's over-the-top, undeserved confidence is more desirable than Prince's insecure, wholly earned arrogance. "The Kid" knows he's the best artist in town, but he's shackled by a fear of failure and a paradoxical desire to have his avant-garde pop accepted by the mainstream; like the man he's based upon, The Kid needs other people to affirm his self-evident greatness. He needs every outsider to tell him what he already knows. But Morris Day is the opposite. How Day views his own ability is irrelevant; he works from a position of limitless self-regard. His confidence is more central to his character than his music or his image.

His confidence *is* his art. He needs no love, because he already loves himself. And as much as we like to pretend that narcissism is gross, it doesn't function that way in society (particularly if the person projecting that narcissism has a sense of humor). It scans as charisma. Prince's supernatural genius ends up feeling less enchanting than Day's supercilious hubris.

There was a sequel to *Purple Rain* (written and directed by Prince) that not many people saw and even fewer liked—1990's *Graffiti Bridge*. Both Prince and Day reprise their Minnesotan characters, this time battling over the ownership of local rock clubs and the heart of a New Age poet named Aura (Ingrid Chavez). Morris is as petulant and self-absorbed as ever. Prince consciously positions himself as a Christlike figure emotionally supported by Aura; near the film's conclusion, Aura dies in an inexplicable car accident. This (somehow) convinces Prince and Morris to end their feud. They shake hands in the street. It's almost like Prince realized he could never turn Day into a true villain, so he decided to create a scenario where Morris suddenly changed. But here's the rub: Morris *didn't* change. He won without winning, because winning was irrelevant. He had nothing else to prove.

A lot of unforeseen things happened to television at the turn of the twenty-first century, the strangest being that it actually became great. Nobody really thought much about TV in the 1970s, or even in the early '90s—everyone watched it, but hardly anyone *cared* about it. In 1985, Joyce Carol Oates wrote an essay for *TV Guide* (!) that lauded the value of *Hill Street Blues,* and everyone wondered if she was being perversely hyperbolic. As recently as the grunge era, there remained a bohemian cachet in casually mentioning that you didn't own a TV. But nobody thinks like that anymore. Today, claiming you don't own a TV simply means you're poor (or maybe depressed). In one ten-year span, high-end television usurped the cultural positions of film, rock, and literary fiction. The way people talk about TV radically changed, and so did the way we judged its quality. For example: When consuming TV in 2013, how do you know the program you're watching is supposed to be art? The most important indicator is the network airing it—if it's on HBO, AMC, or FX, the program is prejudged as sophisticated (and must therefore adhere to a higher standard). But a less obvious clue involves the depiction of any characters who sell drugs. If the drug dealers are depicted positively, the show is automatically seen as "realistic" and directed toward a discriminating adult audience. Drug dealers on high-end TV shows are never straight-up bad guys; they are complicated, highly intelligent, and generally sympathetic.

This is new.

Certainly, there's a long history of American theatrical movies in which drug dealers are supposed to be seen as good people, starting with 1969's *Easy Rider*. It was okay to like a drug dealer for two hours, assuming everyone in the building was over the age of eighteen. But this is never how it was in the non-exclusionary, serialized realm of TV. It was possible for *Miami Vice* to paint a narcotics dealer as engaging, but never as moral. The notion of the drug dealer as a nonvillain was a novel, jarring transition that didn't really happen until 2000. This, of course, doesn't mean that *drugs* can be depicted positively, because that's still verboten (except in satire). The consumption of hard drugs cannot be employed into any narrative without negative consequence, and that bias will probably exist forever (a rare exception was HBO's *Six Feet Under,* where accidental Ecstasy ingestion was sometimes employed for comic purpose). Even the consumption of soft drugs is sketchy. Showtime's *Weeds,* a program that promotes marijuana farming, showed its female lead smoking pot only twice during its first seven seasons. Yet the mere existence of *Weeds*—the mere existence of a show in which the suburban protagonist, Nancy Botwin, is both a drug dealer and a good person—illustrates how dramatically the pusher's on-screen perception has inverted. There are still negative feelings about drugs, but not toward the fictional people who sell them. The two best shows of the past fifteen years—HBO's *The Wire* and AMC's *Breaking Bad*—were essentially built on the moral ambiguity of men who sell heroin and methamphetamine.

The drug lords on *The Wire* were criminals, but they had a stricter ethical code than the corrupt police trying to stop them. The most admirable adult in the series was Omar Little, a hyperviolent stickup artist who lived by a code so austere he wouldn't even cuss (in 2012, Barack Obama cited Omar as his favorite *Wire* character, thus making Obama the first sitting president to express admiration for a fictional homosexual who killed dozens of people with a shotgun). The second most admirable citizen of *The Wire* universe was Stringer Bell, a drug dealer who actually attends community college to become a better businessman. (The fact that this character's identity was a composite based on two actual Baltimore drug lords, Stringer Reed and Roland Bell, isn't even factored into the equation.) Walter White, the protagonist on *Breaking Bad,* was consciously designed by show creator Vince Gilligan to evolve from hero to villain as the show's trajectory progressed. But the fact that his evolution occurred while he cooked meth is secondary—in fact, his initial decision to produce drugs was a straightforward act of heroism, committed for the good of his family. His failure is a desire for control.

Now, don't misinterpret what I'm arguing here—I realize these characters *do* murder people, and their involvement in the drug game is the catalyst for those crimes. But it wasn't the underlying cause. The constraints of their illegal profession placed them in situations where killing was unavoidable. If we accept that criminal activity is an extension of social forces beyond any person's control, criminals are judged for their ethics within that sphere; in a way, we stop judging them entirely. We feel for them when they kill, and we understand why it had to happen. We actively want them to get away with murder, because we are on their side. [And I concede that when I write "we" I'm really writing "I"—but I don't think my sentiments fall outside the writers' intent.]

There are two possible explanations for why this happened. The first is creator driven: It's possible that the people writing these shows simply decided to humanize drug dealers, and—because these shows were successful for all the traditional reasons well-made shows succeed—audiences supported whoever the narrative told them was the hero. Perhaps it's no different from *The Sopranos* or *Dexter,* where people comfortably root for mobsters and serial killers simply because they're the center of the story (and we've all been trained to experience fiction through whichever main character we understand most deeply). But I wonder if part of this isn't coming from the opposite direction. I wonder if this is a way for people (particularly those born in the 1970s) to reconcile the dissonance between what they were told in the 1980s and what they actively experienced in the 1990s. Throughout the '80s, the dangers of drugs were promoted endlessly, most memorably through the "Just Say No" campaign. It was impossible to grow up during that decade without absorbing the omnipresent message that drugs destroyed lives. But then those same kids lived through the '90s, with the added advantage of life experience. They soon realized that PCP didn't always make teenagers jump out of windows and that not everyone who used cocaine turned into Len Bias. They supported a president who smoked marijuana, regardless of his unwillingness to admit inhalation; later, they would vote for a president who admitted snorting blow. This created a jarring cognitive gap: An entire generation had been programmed to fear the very same drugs they came to recognize as mostly innocuous. The stigma of drugs was still hardwired into their worldview, but that stigma was unlike the reality they experienced. From this, an unspoken mental compromise emerged. It was still wrong to lionize drug use, but it was no longer necessary to demonize "drug culture." You could actually *like* drug culture, and you could like the people who lived inside it.

These were people like Stringer Bell and Walter White and Nancy Botwin. Confident people. People with guts who attack hypocrisy and embody pop's truest aphorism: "To live outside the law, you must be honest." That dictum has become the only erudite way to think about fictional drug dealers. As straight-up TV villains, their time has passed. Now they're just complicated versions of hard-working entrepreneurs. They're coal miners. They're farmers.

There's no greater conundrum for the sports-obsessed historian than the relationship between Muhammad Ali and Joe Frazier. It's the most sensitive, least reconcilable schism within the complicated history of race and boxing. It's a contradiction impossible to circumvent: Ali, an athlete whose active role in the history of American race relations looms larger than Jackie Robinson's, consciously committed some of the most egregious acts of racial prejudice in modern sports history, over and over and over again, against someone of his own race (and for no defensible reason).

Everyone who knows anything about Ali is aware of this; it is not some forgotten detail, scrubbed from history. Entire books have been written about the paradox (most notably Mark Kram's *Ghosts of Manila*). HBO produced a documentary on the interpersonal conflict told almost entirely from Frazier's perspective. No credible Ali biographer can ignore it, and no one has ever successfully argued that Ali's rhetoric was taken out of context or exaggerated by his critics. It's just a discomfiting fact about his life: Ali used racial invective to humiliate Frazier and turn African-American fans against him. He pretty much ruined Joe Frazier's life.

Yet this has not diminished Ali's legacy in any consequential way.

It has not damaged his cultural memory. It's the darkest footnote to his professional career, but certainly not a body blow; with every passing year, the shadow of Ali's stature grows. He remains a civil rights icon, and any suggestion to the contrary would be wrong. Ali was polarizing in 1970, but he's not polarizing now.

He's an unassailable cultural character. (In fact, simply including Ali in this book may prompt some to call me racist.) And this forces an inescapable question with no clear answer: Why have we collectively decided that Ali's inexcusable treatment of Frazier is something we'll (pretty much) excuse entirely?

The details of their relationship do not help Ali's case.

Ali and Frazier fought three times: 1971's "Fight of the Century" in Madison Square Garden (decisively won by Frazier), 1974's less memorable rematch (decisively won by Ali), and the 1975 "Thrilla in Manila" in the Philippines, widely cited as the greatest heavyweight battle in history (Ali escaped with a TKO when Frazier's trainer refused to allow a nearly blind Frazier to enter the fifteenth round). Devoid of all social implications, these three fights would still constitute the apex of twentieth-century pugilism. But it was what happened outside the ring that makes this rivalry important to people who don't even care about boxing. The two enemies began as allies, engrossed with identical goals; when Ali was banned from boxing in 1967 for refusing military service, Frazier petitioned Nixon for Ali's reinstatement and privately gave his exiled friend financial assistance. At the time, they were more similar than different. They needed each other. But that relationship ended the moment their collision became imminent. Under the guise of prefight publicity, Ali leveled racially infused attacks on Frazier's intellect that framed Frazier as a stereotype and an extension of white America. "Boxers like Joe Frazier have no imagination," Ali said. "He's just a flat-nosed, ugly pug. He's just an athlete. He can't talk about nothing." Most memorably, Ali ceaselessly compared Frazier to a gorilla. What's difficult to understand is the way Ali was somehow able to paint Frazier as both subhuman and less authentically black. In 1974, on the BBC talk show *Parkinson,* Ali said Frazier was "the other type of Negro . . . he works for the enemy." On a technical level, Ali was (probably) referring to the organization that backed Frazier financially, a predominantly white investment collective from Philadelphia called Cloverlay. But such an implication contradicted the totality of Frazier's life: He'd been raised in poverty on a cotton and watermelon farm in rural South Carolina (and until his death in 2011, he still lived in a tiny apartment inside a gym in one of the blackest sections of Philadelphia). There isn't *anything* about Joe Frazier that suggests he was disrespectful, uninterested, or even vaguely uncomfortable with his racial identity. But this did not matter. By the time they fought in '71, Frazier was seen as a black man fighting for white interests. The onslaught continued immediately after Frazier won the fight, a unanimous decision Ali refused to recognize: "White people say I lost."

Now, it would be wrong to casually discount the legitimacy of Ali's feelings on these issues. His courage cannot be questioned. Ali always went all the way: When pressed over his unwillingness to fight in the Vietnam War due to his pacifist Muslim beliefs, he flatly stated, "Even if it means facing machine gun fire, I'll face it before denouncing Elijah Muhammad and the religion of Islam. I'm ready to die." He was not speaking metaphorically. Part of the reason we want to forgive him is that he spoke with so much electrifying conviction. But few people are willing to recognize just how *out there* Ali was in the 1970s. Before the 1975 fight in Manila, Ali bragged about attending a Ku Klux Klan meeting; he met with the KKK's leadership because they agreed on the issue of interracial marriage (both sides saw it as an atrocity). The meeting was set up by Ali's financial (and intellectual) backers, the Nation of Islam. This detail cannot be tossed aside: *Muhammad Ali met with the KKK because he thought they had some good ideas.* That's as radical as radical gets. Today it's common to hear members of the media bemoan how we don't have athletes as politically aware as Muhammad Ali, and that's totally true. But how, exactly, would ESPN react if someone like Cam Newton casually mentioned that he shared some common ground with the Aryan Brotherhood? It would be (ahem) "a problem." But this bizarre historical footnote has not damaged Ali; in fact, it generally seems more interesting than troubling. No one factors it into Ali's iconography, in the same way that Beatles fans choose not to accept the long-standing rumors of John Lennon's abusive relationships with women. In many ways, it illuminates the core of Ali's media brilliance. The reason his ill-advised missteps were eliminated from the conversation is not that Ali managed to convince the white working class to support Frazier; it's that Ali made the intellectual class of white America believe that siding with unenlightened pro-Frazier rednecks meant they were retrograde intellectuals. Ali presented every idea—good or bad—as essential human truth, and he succeeded through sheer force of personality.

Everyone knows history is written by the winners, but that cliché misses a crucial detail: Over time, the winners are *always* the progressives. Conservatism can only win in the short term, because society cannot stop evolving (and social evolution inevitably dovetails with the agenda of those who see change as an abstract positive). It might take seventy years, but it always happens eventually. Serious historians are, almost without exception, self-styled progressives. Radical views—even the awful ones—improve with age. What Ali managed to do was make the media cognizant of the future within the present tense. He presented "Ali/Frazier" as an inflexible dichotomy in which he was always the progressive, regardless of the facts. It did not matter that he saw social value in the separation of races; it did not matter that Frazier's life experience personified the underclass Ali claimed to champion. To disagree with Ali was to disagree with social advancement, and if this felt contradictory . . . well, then, you clearly didn't understand the conflict. How could any intellectual dispute Ali's insights on race? Did they not know who he was and what he had gone through? "Joe Frazier's just an ordinary individual," Ali reminded them. "He doesn't represent anything." Here again, it all comes down to confidence: Ali had proven himself as radical and defined himself as meaningful. Siding with

Frazier in 1972 was siding with the wrong side of history *in real time*. And once the intellectual class embraced that perspective, they never retreated. The passing of time only cements that certitude. They need their memory to correspond with reality, so they establish a reality that's new.

In Ali's defense, it must be noted that he apologized for his treatment of Frazier, privately to Frazier's son Marvis and publicly in a 2001 edition of the *New York Times* (although, curiously, never to Joe himself). There are other mitigating factors to consider, most notably Ali's age, his education, and the amount of control the Nation of Islam held over him. (Some of Ali's most famous quotations—including the sublime "No Vietcong ever called me Nigger"—were directly fed to him by other people.) If we objectively balance the good things Ali did against the bad, there's no question he's ultimately heroic. But that's not the issue. The issue is that these kinds of questions are *never* weighed objectively. That's not how the court of public opinion operates. It's easy to think of iconic figures who lived mostly moral lives, only to have their legacy obliterated by one fatal mistake. Considering the irony of this particular conflict, it seems like this error could have devastated the perception of Ali. It seems like something people would never forget, and (I suppose) this essay proves that some people haven't. People remember. But they don't care, because Ali was too "Ali." He convinced the world that his statements were always politically justified, even when they weren't. He was too confident to question. We had to let it go.

I am of the opinion that D. B. Cooper fell from the sky and died on impact. There's nothing to suggest he survived and a lot of evidence suggesting he did not, most notably the 1980 discovery of $5,800 in the Columbia River (it was found by an eight-year-old boy, and the serial numbers on the deteriorating currency identified it as part of Cooper's ransom). Of course, the discovery of that money had the reverse effect on Cooper superfans, some of whom insist that Cooper consciously planted the $5,800 in the water to make people *think* he died. [And this, of course, is the central problem with conspiracy theorists—once you inflexibly accept that something is a conspiracy, any contrary evidence has the paradoxical effect of making your case stronger. Every contradiction deepens the conspiracy. I suppose this axiom doesn't perfectly apply to the Cooper case, because this isn't a "conspiracy" in the classic sense—no one views it as a governmental cover-up. But it's a case of insane wish fulfillment, which operates in almost the same way. The role of the government is simply replaced with anyone rational.]

Still, I would like to believe that D. B. Cooper is alive. I like to imagine him living on the beach in Cabo, somehow subsisting on the $194,200 he didn't ingeniously plant in the river to throw off the Feds. There's a community in Washington (a town called Ariel, population 870) that commemorates the 1971 air crime every November, which is not that distant from celebrating a prison break or a bank heist. But it *feels* distant, and everyone accepts that feeling as reasonable. You simply don't find people interested in this case who don't side with Cooper. He's something that can't exist in the modern present: the universally beloved hijacker.

In the weeks following the September 11, 2001, attacks on the World Trade Center and the Pentagon, it became common to classify the suicidal terrorists as "cowards." George W. Bush called them this directly, and others have continued to reinforce the sentiment. ("For seven years, I have marveled at the utter cowardice of the 9/11 hijackers," declared CNN's Gary Tuchman on the attack's 2008 anniversary.) The language was a conscious, semantic counterattack; Bush specifically chose the word *cowardice* for its loaded Islamic connotation: "The most evil [traits] in a man are severe stinginess and uninhibited cowardice," states the prophet Muhammad in a collection of platitudes titled *Sunan Abu Dawud*. [Semi-related: I find it amusing that this document places "stinginess" on par with "cowardice."] To a much larger degree, it was just a backward way of thinking about what happened on that September morning. Killing yourself for political reasons is stupid and unjustified, but it's certainly not cowardly. It's the opposite of cowardly. Still, this became the default way to present the character of the 9/11 terrorists (so much so that comedian Bill Maher lost his job at ABC for pointing out the linguistic hypocrisy). In general, anything involving suicide (terroristic or otherwise) is tagged as "cowardly" and "selfish." Yet here we have Cooper—a man who put the lives of private citizens at risk for nothing except money—and he gets tagged as *bold*. He's an anti-authoritarian ballbreaker, referenced in Kid Rock songs and appreciated by everyone who's able to remember who he was. The takeaway is not just that D. B. Cooper is not a villain; the takeaway is that what D. B. Cooper attempted is actively perceived as *good*.

Now, I'm not trying to argue that Cooper and Mohamed Atta are ultimately the same. They are fundamentally different. But that shouldn't make them opposites, because they do share a massive similarity. They're both defined by the decision to hijack an airplane, so they should both exist on similar tiers of distaste: Atta should obviously be hated *more*, but Cooper should be hated *some*. It seems like hijacking a plane is reason enough to vilify someone, and the level of villainy should mostly come down to motive; in other words, wanting to kill strangers and annihilate secular society is worse than the desire for unearned money. But neither option should be a net positive. D. B. Cooper knew the most (about airline protocol and skydiving) and cared the least (about his safety and the safety of others). He should be a villain. But that overlooks the one intangible that makes Americans forgive everything else: superhuman self-assurance. The motive for a hijacking matters, but not as much as the execution. Cooper had verve. In the same way that people who kill themselves are denigrated for wanting to die, he is exonerated for assuming he could easily survive. He believed he could make outrageous demands that the airline would accept; he believed he could parachute from a commercial airplane in the middle of the night; he believed he would avoid the inevitable nationwide manhunt and never be found. The fact that he believed all this while remaining "a gentleman" makes him historically indestructible. Is there anything more attractive than a polite person with limitless self-belief? There is not. Avoiding villainy is not that different from avoiding loneliness: First, you must love yourself. And if you do that convincingly enough, others will love you too much.

EASIER THAN TYPING

Let's pretend Batman is real.

[I'm aware that this opening is enough to stop a certain kind of person from reading any further. It could be the opening line from an episode of *Community* that references a previous episode of *Community*. But that's life. That's how it goes.]

Let's pretend Batman is real. Let's assume Gotham City is the real New York, and someone is suddenly skulking the streets at night, inexplicably dressed like a winged mammal. (For the sake of argument, we're also assuming this is happening in a universe where the preexisting Batman™ character has never been invented by DC Comics, so no one is presuming that this is a person *impersonating* Batman—this is an original Batman, within a world where he's never been previously imagined. It's also happening within our current reality, so supervillains don't exist.) He has an amazing car, a willingness to engage in street violence, and no affiliations with any traditional authority. He is, however, driven by the same interior motives as the conventional comic book character: Having seen his parents murdered, a super-rich orphan decides to dedicate himself to crime fighting. But *you*, of course, don't know those dark details. This scenario has just emerged from the ether. There's no preexisting backstory. No one knows anything about who this Bat Person is or what he hopes to accomplish. We are all learning about Batman in real time; every detail about his life is presented as new information.

You first hear about Batman anecdotally. At a dinner party,

59

someone tells a story he'd heard from someone at his office: A young woman was being gang-raped in the Bronx, but a costumed stranger swooped in and beat the criminals senseless. Or maybe you heard the same story in a different way; maybe you hear about a mother whose teenage son ended up in the hospital after a man dressed like a winged mammal broke his jaw. (In this version of the confrontation, the hospitalized teen was innocently hanging out with his friends and flirting with a promiscuous girl they all knew from school.) A few weeks later, you hear another story from a more trustworthy acquaintance you are inclined to believe—he claims he was walking home from a tavern in Brooklyn when he saw a man wearing a cape jumping between the roofs of two tall buildings. Soon after, everyone in the city seems to be obsessing over this unknown Bat Person, sometimes gravely but often ironically. He is constantly trending on Twitter.

While taking a train uptown, you see subway graffiti spouting obtuse slogans like BATMAN DESTROYS. There's a local TV news report in which policemen are interviewed about the rumor of a man dressed like a bat protecting the ghettos; the cops insist that vigilantism is wrong and that this person is dangerous (if he even exists, which remains unproven). The *New York Post* publishes the first mainstream story about Batman: They love him (an editorial half-jokingly urges him to become *more* violent). The *Village Voice* responds to the *Post*'s depiction, satirizing Batman as a homoerotic cross between Mike Tyson and Rudy Giuliani. The *New York Times* publishes a short online story that strongly implies Batman is an urban myth. The *New York Daily News* presents a series of detailed, semi-gratuitous examples of how the buzz around Batman is changing crime patterns in the metro area. Eventually, an irrefutable video of Batman is captured on someone's iPhone and streamed on numerous websites. Soon after, the *New York Times* concedes that Batman is real; it labels him as "a criminal outlier." A Fox News pundit nationalizes the story, arguing that the existence of a Batman proves that Democratic leadership is failing the American people. Conspiracy theories suggest Batman was created by the CIA in order to undermine the Occupy Wall Street movement. Media bloggers are convinced this is all an advertising campaign for a yet-to-be-released sports drink. The *New York Observer* examines his role as a burgeoning fashion icon. Soon after, Batman murders an unarmed man in public, seemingly at random; when authorities search the victim's apartment, they find evidence linking the dead man to a ring of child pornographers. Public opinion continues to splinter. Because he wears a ridiculous costume and cannot be captured, most informed citizens come to a collection of related conclusions: This so-called "Batman"—whoever he is and whatever he hopes to achieve—is brilliant, brutal, insane, capricious, unwilling to compromise, and obsessed with the criminal underworld.

But here again . . . this is *all* you know.

The only things you know about Batman are what you've heard through gossip or gleaned from the media (so you really don't know anything). Divorce yourself from the fact that you already believe Batman is a heroic figure. Don't think about Adam West or Michael Keaton. Don't imagine yourself as a citizen of Christopher Nolan's Gotham; imagine yourself *as yourself.* Try to pretend that all you know about this figure is what you've just read in the previous three paragraphs. You don't know that he's secretly a millionaire. You don't know what his motives are. All you know is what you read in the papers.

Do you root for this person, or do you want him arrested?

Bernhard Goetz was not Batman. This should be obvious, particularly since Batman is not widely perceived as a squirrel-obsessed racist. The person Bernhard Goetz is more often compared to is Paul Kersey, the character portrayed by Charles Bronson in the *Death Wish* movies: After the murder of his wife and the rape of his daughter, Kersey (a reformed pacifist) walks around the worst parts of Nixon-era New York in the hope of being mugged; whenever it happens, he shoots his attackers dead. This modus operandi prompts a fundamental question about passive-aggressive victimhood: If you *want* to be attacked, are you still a victim? I'm sure Goetz would say yes. He'd also argue that no one ever "wants" to be attacked, and that his actions were simply the inevitable, unfortunate result of a city's failure to keep its populace safe (so perhaps he has more in common with Batman than we want to believe, at least within my projection of his mind).

"I wanted to kill those guys. I wanted to maim those guys. I wanted to make them suffer in every way I could." This was Goetz speaking in the hours after his surrender and arrest on the last day of 1984. The "guys" Goetz was referring to were four black teenagers who (probably) tried to mug him on the downtown number 2 express train in Manhattan. I use the word *probably* because there are some who'd argue that the four youths were mere panhandlers who had politely asked Goetz for five dollars without any threat of violence, even though they all had minor police records (and despite the fact that one of them would later admit they were probably going to rob him). The four teens walked toward Goetz and requested/demanded money; Goetz pulled out an unlicensed .38 caliber handgun and shot all four, right there in the subway car. (In a 1996 interview, he claimed this act was "easier than typing.") All four survived, although one took a bullet in the spinal cord and was paralyzed for life. Goetz, by his own admission, was pretty ruthless: "If I had more bullets, I would have shot 'em all again and again. My problem was I ran out of bullets." He also says he considered gouging one of the victims' eyes out with his apartment key, a resolutely un-Batmanlike move.

The shooting occurred on the afternoon of December 22, 1984. After briefly talking to the other (now terrified) passengers and the train's baffled conductor, Goetz exited the subway and spent the next nine days in a rental car, driving around New England and staying in various hotels under false names (always paying cash). For some reason, he returned to New York on the thirtieth, rented a different car, and proceeded to drive to Concord, New Hampshire. He turned himself in to Concord authorities the next day. Examining the video footage of his first police interview is like watching a mumblecore Mamet play: With oversize eyeglasses and the receding hair of a man who is no longer concerned with vanity, Goetz describes the subway shooting with a clinical directness that seems almost rehearsed (but not quite). "I was just whistling Dixie, okay? I was in fear. And that's good, because that helps you think. That helps you think. But when I saw [one of the muggers'] eyes, my state of mind changed and you go through a different state of mind where reality totally, totally changes."

It is rare that anyone truly becomes an "overnight" celebrity, but this is one example in which that cliché is pretty much true. Goetz instantly became an international metaphor. Though it would be an overstatement to claim initial support for the shooting was universal, it was close: In the mid-eighties, New York was a simmering cesspool. It was a terrible place to live, unless you were a millionaire or a criminal (or, I suppose, an artist). There were roughly fifteen hundred metro murders every year; New York's crime rate was 70 percent higher than the rest of the country's. The possibility that someone would respond to a violent culture with extreme prejudice seemed problematic, but not unjust or unreasonable. Writing about the incident for *New York* magazine decades later, social critic/jazz writer Stanley Crouch made it seem as if absolutely no one was against the vigilante: "It may be almost impossible for someone who did not live in New York twenty years ago to understand the first few days of spiritual uplift that followed the incident that made Bernhard Goetz famous . . . The shooting brought about an enormous shift of mood. In so many telephone conversations and exchanges in bars, on street corners, in beauty parlors, in pool halls, and wherever each version of particular people met, from the too rich to the very poor, there was a collective emotion that cannot be described as anything other than jubilant." This is possibly (perhaps probably) true. But the more people learned about the case, the more their favor drifted away from Goetz's corner. Certainly, his own attitude made things worse for himself—at one point he told a reporter the paralyzed victim would have been better off if he'd been aborted by his mother. Strong rumors suggested that the half-Jewish Goetz had casually made racist comments at a community meeting eighteen months before the shooting. Though Goetz claimed to be confused and uncomfortable with his sudden fame, his posture suggested that he liked and craved the attention; more important, he never showed authentic remorse for anything that happened.

By the summer of 1985, two dominant (and somewhat predictable) views on the confrontation had emerged: Right-leaning people saw the shooting as justified, while Left-leaning people felt Goetz was more of a criminal than the teens he shot. A headline in *People* magazine from that winter could not have been more evenhanded: HE ACTED OUT OUR ANGRIEST FANTASIES, BUT A YEAR LATER THE QUESTIONS REMAIN: IS HE A HERO OR A VILLAIN, A VICTIM OR A CRIMINAL? Those positions still (vaguely) exist today, at least among older New York residents who remember the incident firsthand. But such ethical confusion has generally eroded over time, at least within the media community. Virtually no one "debates" Goetz anymore. The two most common views are not balanced: The first is a total surprise that the event happened at all (it's difficult for young Manhattanites to imagine a not-so-distant era when subways were dangerous). The second, more universal view is a reflexive assumption that Goetz was obviously and irrefutably wrong. Easy evidence of this can be seen in the headline from the aforementioned Crouch essay, published in 2003: THE JOY OF GOETZ: THERE WAS A MOMENT IN BULLIED-BY-THUGS, PRE-RUDY NEW YORK

WHEN EVEN THIS CREEP WAS A HERO. At this point, feigned objectivity is unnecessary.

There are almost no Goetz supporters in the modern age. He still has a modicum of notoriety, but his stature is unserious. When he inexplicably ran for mayor in 2001, he received only a thousand votes (about four hundred fewer than Kenny Kramer, a man exclusively known for inspiring Michael Richards's character on the sitcom *Seinfeld*). Still, he never went to jail, which is really what matters: Goetz was found not guilty in the criminal trial, escaping the charge of attempted murder. In essence, the jury decided his 1984 actions on the train fell within the boundaries of self-defense as dictated by the state of New York. The statute states that responding with deadly force is acceptable if a citizen "reasonably believes that such other person is committing or attempting to commit" a serious crime against him. Eleven years after his acquittal, Goetz lost the inevitable civil trial and was supposed to pay the paralyzed victim (Darrel Cabey) $43 million. Goetz immediately filed for bankruptcy and still claims to have paid nothing. When covering the latter trial, the *New York Times* mentioned that the criminal jury had been predominately white, while the civil jury was predominately black and Latino. Also noted was the fact that six members of the criminal jury had themselves been crime victims.

In the years that have passed, the (always pretty strange) Goetz has grown progressively more bizarre. He continued to live a solitary life in New York. He became a militant vegetarian and an outspoken advocate for the New York squirrel population, rescuing (and sometimes sharing his tiny apartment with) the bushy-tailed rodents. He opened a small electronics store and brazenly named it Vigilante Electronics. He granted a TV interview to former *Star Trek* star William Shatner. Life has gone less smoothly for the four teenagers he shot; all were eventually convicted of crimes and one of them committed suicide (that was James Ramseur, who killed himself after spending twenty-five years in prison for raping and sodomizing a pregnant woman less than two years after being shot in the subway).

Goetz is not always hated, but he is consistently categorized as hateful. Sometimes you'll stumble across an aging Goetz sympathizer who'll argue that life was "different" in 1984 and that the city was truly under siege, but even those apologists feel obligated to note that Goetz is a nutcase. His main role is that of a footnote—the discomfiting face of eighties urban violence.

So . . . Goetz is a villain. We accept this, and the passage of time will turn that consensus into concrete. If Goetz was still at large and Batman was somehow real, we'd have to assume Batman would be trying to stop him. We concede they would be adversaries. And this dissonance illustrates a central paradox of the human mind: When considering the vigilante, the way we think about fiction contradicts how we feel about reality. Which should not be unanticipated or confusing, yet somehow always is.

Let's jump back to *Death Wish*, a melodrama falling somewhere between the totally real (Goetz) and the obviously fake (Batman). Directed by British archconservative Michael Winner, the 1974 film was based on a 1972 novel of the same title written by Brian Garfield. The respective plots are similar, but their central morals are not. The book argues against the concept of vigilantism and focuses on the protagonist's moral confusion; the movie celebrates the vigilante and makes him an anonymous hero. It was a creative evolution that (predictably) bothered Garfield. But that evolution was soon reversed by the media, since virtually every film critic who's ever written about the celluloid version of *Death Wish* uses it as a means for attacking reactionary politics. At every turn, the polarity of the message was inverted: Garfield wrote a novel that was *against* an idea, which was misinterpreted by Winner as being *for* an idea, which was then received as proof of a flawed ideology. As a means for forwarding progressive ideas, Garfield's anti-vigilante book was less successful than the angry response to the pro-vigilante movie it paradoxically inspired. In every medium and context, *Death Wish* makes its audience prone to disagree with whatever they think they're being told directly.

Death Wish is a "New York movie," which means audiences in New York get to feel interesting whenever they recognize geographical locations they typically ignore from the back of a taxi. Its visual images of the decaying city make seventies New York appear unlivable—it resembles a dirty, sci-fi dystopia slowly collapsing under the idealistic failure of the sixties. Bronson's character Paul Kersey (whom I will refer to as "Bronson" from here on out because, really, that's how we would refer to him in any normal conversation about the film) is an architect. In the second scene, while discussing the city's escalating crime rate with his coworkers, he is directly referred to as "a bleeding-heart liberal." After his wife's murder and the unorthodox rape of his daughter (spearheaded by a nonfamous Jeff Goldblum in his first film role), Bronson finds himself more confused than despondent. The whole world seems different. He starts to notice the reality of his vulnerability. He fills one of his dress socks with twenty-dollars' worth of quarters and nails a mugger in the face. It feels good. His architecture job requires him to travel to Tucson, described by a local as "gun country." We subsequently learn that Bronson was a conscientious objector during the Korean War, the manifestation of his long-standing pacifism inspired by his father's death in a deer-hunting accident. Nonetheless, his host in Arizona surreptitiously gives him a handgun as a going-away present for his return to New York; soon after, Bronson is walking through Riverside Park alone at night, waiting to be assaulted. When it finally happens, he shoots the criminal in the gut. At first, the violence sickens him: He rushes back to his apartment and pukes in the toilet. But this remorse is fleeting. A night later, he stumbles across three more criminals (this time beating a random stranger) and murders all three, shooting one mugger in the back while he flees over a fence. A few days later, he kills two more thugs on the subway, discharging bullets into their bleeding bodies as they lie prone on the floor of the train, just as Goetz would do to Darrel Cabey in 1984.

"What are we," Bronson's character rhetorically asks his son-in-law, Jack, after visiting his catatonic daughter. Like the rest of the city, Jack has no idea that his wife's father is the (now famous, yet unknown) vigilante. "What have we become? What do you call people who—when faced with a condition of fear—do nothing about it? Who just run and hide?"

"Civilized," counters the son-in-law.

"No," says Bronson.

And that's all he says: *No*. Which ends up being more effective than any aphoristic retort a more creative screenwriter might have tried. His understated, monosyllabic message is that urban crime is the unavoidable manifestation of a modern society in which being "civilized" is the default value setting. It's not that Charles Bronson is an uncivilized person; it's more that he believes the obligations of civility are limited to the civilized world. The uncivil receive no quarter. This, for most people, is the central debate within *Death Wish*: Is it acceptable to behave like a criminal in order to stop crime?

If you loathe the sensationalism of *Death Wish*, the mere existence of that question troubles you. But there's something else about this movie that's thornier than any straightforward question over the protagonist's actions, and it has to do with the clarity of his motives. Bronson's pacifism is a result of his father's death; his full-on vigilantism emerges only after his wife and daughter are assaulted. In both cases, extremist views are magically manufactured by specific personal experiences. They are not philosophies. They are visceral responses to painful, unthinkable memories. It's not just that Bronson wouldn't have shot any muggers if his wife and daughter had not been harmed—he would have vehemently disagreed with the very concept of *anyone* behaving in that manner. When he suddenly starts to shoot random stickup artists, he is not following his mind. He is following his heart (or, more accurately, the emotional part of the brain we like to pretend is living in the chest). Within the limited context of the *Death Wish* narrative, this emotive antilogic makes the audience like him more. If *Death Wish* were presented as a comic book, the assault on his family would be classified as Paul Kersey's "origin story." It would be the only moment from his life that really mattered. Audiences instantly relate to the idea of justified revenge, particularly in high-testosterone genres like the western or the urban thriller—it feels more human than supporting a person whose behavior is dictated by a balanced, preexisting, cognitive field theory. We support fictional characters motivated by a need to equalize injustice, regardless of how they go about it (in *Dirty Harry,* Clint Eastwood somehow has the prophetic ability to shoot people *before* they commit crimes). In a movie, such a response always seems reasonable. But that doesn't translate into nonfictional settings. Within the rarefied desert of the real, the bar for what's reasonable is much, much higher.

The story of Batman has been reimagined several times since his 1939 introduction, but the fundamental details have never been altered: As a little boy, Bruce Wayne witnesses the murder of his rich parents, launching his desire to stop all those who make the world unsafe for the innocent. Because he has no superpowers, was born rich, and generally seems like a pretty haunted dude, Batman completists like to dwell on the pathos of The Bat. Yet the most glaring element of this pathos—a word deriving from the Greek terms for "suffering" and "experience"—is ignored out of necessity: Batman never questions the logic of letting a childhood experience dictate his entire life.

Here again, let's work from the premise that Batman is real: At the age of eight, he sees his parents killed by a thug. Certainly, this kind of incident would affect his worldview. One might argue that such trauma could stunt a person's emotional maturation and stop him from becoming a whole person. Still, we all know that Bruce Wayne is not retarded. He couldn't succeed at his mission if he wasn't self-aware. He has an understanding of social norms and a grasp on human psychology. He's a troubled—but still thoughtful—figure. Yet Batman never tries to overcome this childhood event. It becomes the only meaningful moment of his entire history, and he doesn't seem to question why this is the case. "I think the refusal to examine the insanity of what he's doing is the whole point of Batman," argues culture writer Alex Pappademas, paraphrasing the sentiments of *Batman* screenwriter Sam Hamm. "He's a rich solipsist who can never beat up enough muggers to bring his dead parents back. But because he's a billionaire, he can afford to keep trying forever. He's never confronted with the futility of what he's doing. Were he to examine and work past those motivations, you'd have no story. The guy has to stay broken."

In fiction, we tend to isolate and amplify one aspect of a man's life into his entire subconscious. Batman experienced a singular, personal trauma that made him want to protect the rest of society for the remainder of his life. The same thing happens to Bronson in *Death Wish*—the link between his familial trauma and his subsequent vigilantism is seen as an acceptable narrative extension; what outraged critics is not that Bronson's character killed criminals, but that he grew to enjoy it (and continued to do so throughout four less-nuanced sequels). In the unreal world, a vigilante is heroic. And that's because he is motivated *by only one thing*. Event A creates behavior B. We perceive and connect those two acts in a vacuum, and that makes them philosophically equal (even if the depth of the vigilantism far exceeds the initial wrong).

Bernhard Goetz was a hero as long as no one knew anything about him. During the week he remained at large, he was consumed by the public as a fictional, binary character: an attacked man who attacked back. Was it unusual that he happened to be riding the subway with a gun? Well, yes. But the fact that he had to use it proved that it was necessary. Did it seem curious that he shot people who *didn't* have guns? Perhaps. But how was he to know they didn't at least have knives (or, as was later erroneously reported, sharpened screwdrivers)? There was nothing else known about this person, so his motives could be attributed only to whatever might have occurred on that train (a confrontation any normal person would envision as terrifying, and that a less than normal person might imagine as a deeply satisfying fantasy). Within a limited reality, Goetz wins by forfeit. Vigilantism's profound contradiction is that every socially aware person agrees that it cannot be allowed to exist, even though huge swaths of society would improve if it sometimes did. As long as Goetz remained a nameless, faceless "concept," those two incongruous realities were in equilibrium.

But then Goetz became real. He was not merely a problem of democracy; he was a thin man in a leather jacket without remorse. And from the moment that transformation happened, people started to turn on him.

They could just tell he was weird.

That, I realize, is an oversimplification (and maybe even a cheap shot). It wasn't like the world saw Goetz's angular face and instantly decided to hate him; comedian Joan Rivers even sent him a telegram and offered to pay his bail. The fact that he wasn't handsome didn't help his cause, but that wasn't what marginalized him; he theoretically could have used it to his public advantage, had he portrayed himself as an altruistic nerd. He had a traumatic encounter to balance his aggression—in 1981, Goetz was injured when three teenagers mugged him in the subway—and a scarred personal history that could have justified his twisted intensity (when he was twelve, Goetz's father pleaded guilty to molestation charges). Had Bernhard Goetz somehow managed to limit the public's understanding of his life to those two particulars, it's possible he would have remained a folk hero forever. What he should have said to the world is this: "I know how it feels to be scared and I know how it feels to be hurt, and I didn't want anyone else to have those feelings just because they went out in public." If he could have contained the public understanding of his persona—if he could have painted the subway shooting and his own personal trauma as a one-to-one relationship, and if he'd convincingly insisted it was done for the benefit of random strangers—he likely would have become a superhero. "Civilized" society would still have expressed abstract distaste for the vigilante theory, but it could have embraced the lone vigilante who risked his own life for the lives of others (just as we do with Batman). But here's the thing: Batman is cool. And more important, Batman is fake. He can't be investigated by reporters. Nobody from the *New York Times* is going to find out that Batman once referenced "niggers and spics" at a community-watch meeting. Batman can't naïvely agree to talk with a journalist and carelessly outline his personal politics, only to see his words reduced and recast as empathy-free arrogance. Because he is unreal, Batman controls the Batman Message. He lives in a finite unreality. Goetz faced (and partially created) the opposite circumstance. Every forthcoming detail about his life—even the positive ones—made his actions on the subway seem *too personal*. And people hate that. What people appreciate are scenarios in which someone's individual experience becomes universal. When that transference goes the other way—when something wholly universal (like the fear of crime) comes across as highly personalized (as it did for Goetz)—the ultimate takeaway is revulsion. It seems pathetic and unreasonable. It seems like the behavior of a person who wants attention at any cost.

Goetz talked too much. He tried to own his persona, and that made everything worse, as it always does. This was his fatal flaw, more than the accusations of racism or his unsexy face or his bloodlust on the train. People could have gotten over all those things. They would have fabricated their own justifications and excuses. But Americans can't get over the idea of a man who unsuccessfully aspires to be what he is not—in this case, a reasonable man who wasn't overjoyed about finding an opportunity to shoot someone he'd never met. Goetz did not understand why people liked him before they knew who he was. He did not realize that the public's positive image of his personality was constructed only because they knew nothing about his true makeup. He decided to let the world see him as more than a one-dimensional character, and that never helps anyone who's already famous. He should have said nothing. He should have said zero about who he was or what he truly believed, just like Bruce Wayne or Charles Bronson.

I'm not the first person who has ever drawn lines between Goetz, Batman, and Bronson. I've never had an idea that a hundred other people didn't have before me. The day after the shooting, the link between the subway assassin and the premise of *Death Wish* was so palpable (and the actual details so murky) that *Death Wish* was the only way most journalists could explain it. The Goetz-as-Batman conceit emerged more slowly. Prolific sci-fi novelist Norman Spinrad considers (and discounts) the idea of "Batman as a Grand Guignol Bernhard Goetz" in a nonfiction work titled *Science Fiction in the Real World*. An academic named Tim Blackmore has also considered Batman as a Goetz figure, noting that both characters embody French political scientist Alexis de Tocqueville's fear that "democracy will transmute itself into authoritarianism." But oddly—or maybe predictably—most of those comparisons are primarily occupied with why everyone still loves Batman (as opposed to why everyone stopped loving Goetz). They start from the premise that vigilantism is indisputably wrong. The core question is always some version of "Why are actions unacceptable in life somehow acceptable in fiction?" But this seems like the wrong thing to worry about. That answer seems self-evident. I more often wonder about the reverse: Why are the qualities we value in the unreal somehow verboten in reality?

I realize the language of those two sentences is similar. However, the problems are very different. The reason things unacceptable in life are acceptable in fiction is because fiction is often the only way we can comfortably examine the morally obscene. For example, we can't *really* understand the interior mind of a serial killer like Ted Bundy. It's impossible. We can barely understand the mind of the sane. Moreover, dwelling on Bundy's motives is (arguably) insulting to the people he murdered. It makes a killer into an artist. Taking Bundy seriously as a rational thinker ends up "making the perpetrator superior to the victim," argues *Popular Crime* author Bill James. "The reason the rest of us don't act on our worst impulses is because we care about the people who would be our victims. Ted Bundy did not care. Trying to see things his way is to depersonalize his victims and to not care about them."

I don't necessarily agree with this point in totality, but I see the logic; James is suggesting that it's socially inappropriate to try and understand the (obviously depraved) mind of a real killer, because that kind of detached rumination is offensive to the real people he harmed. His victims shouldn't be mere footnotes. However, this *can* be done in transgressive fiction. As long as he's not real, a madman's interior process can be manipulated and dissected without consequence. There are no real victims to respect. It's a way for average people to think about the unthinkable. Most open-minded people can read the Bret Easton Ellis novel *American Psycho* and enjoy it as a thought experiment, even when the experimental thoughts are disturbing and depraved. You're not supposed to like or understand the person you're reading about. You're not even supposed to like or understand the author. Patrick Bateman, the central character in *American Psycho,* is depicted as charming and urbane—but he's not supposed to seem that way to the person reading the book. Bateman's personality is to be taken as charming and urbane *to other fictional entities* who don't know who he actually is, all of whom are living inside Bret Easton Ellis's *fictional world*. The audience is involved, but just barely (which is what the critics never understood). Fiction is a type of one-way entertainment. This is not an especially complex phenomenon: We can appreciate detestable things in fiction because those detestable things didn't happen to anyone who's actually alive. It's as straightforward as that. A child can understand it.

The reverse, however, is harder to comprehend. It's difficult to understand why people only support certain *desirable* things if they remain unreal. Yet it happens all the time, and especially with depictions of vigilantes. Batman is a beloved fictional figure who would not be beloved in a nonfictional world, even if the real-life version was identical to his fabricated image in every conceivable way. He would be seen as a brutal freak, scarier to the public than the criminals he captured. *We would not believe he was good.* We would believe his thirst for justice was a disarticulation of his own sick psychology. Batman is not a superhero because of his physical abilities and mental acuities; Batman is a superhero because he seems like a moral impossibility. No one believes a real human would live that far outside the law for the good of other people. His altruistic motives are plausible only in a fake world.

Like I said before—Bernhard Goetz was not Batman. But it wouldn't have mattered if he were. As a framework for living, we have collectively agreed that violently responding to crime makes society worse, which means the person who does so must be viewed as a self-interested criminal. Street justice is a desirable fantasy, but it must remain a fantasy in order for the desire to exist. In a book or a movie, the vigilante cares about us. In life, he cares more about the squirrels. It's the only way.

HUMAN CLAY

"The culture is coarsening."

I have placed the above phrase in quote marks, as if someone specific has said it directly. It certainly would not be difficult to find someone who has. But what would that prove? I'm not trying to suggest that this is any kind of combustive, uncommon opinion. It's a given. Sometimes a contrarian will try to dispute the sentiment, usually with an abstract argument about how civilized our modernity seems when compared to the Crusades or the Roman empire or pre-LBJ Mississippi, and—technically—that's true. We no longer watch people kill themselves for pleasure, unless you count pro football. But that's not what normal people mean when they lament the coarsening of the culture. It has nothing to do with actual violence or an erosion of fundamental morals. When people say the culture is coarsening, they're ostensibly arguing that what is totally acceptable now would have been only marginally acceptable ten years ago and virtually unmentionable twenty-five years before that. It's not really about people's private behavior or personal taste, because that doesn't change much; it's more a statement about what's tolerable to talk about in public during daylight hours. The historical arc of MTV is an easy way to see this evolution. The way people argue on FOX and MSNBC is another, as is pretty much the entire lifespan of the Internet. As an all-purpose semantic rule, the culture *is* coarsening. It's not an unreasonable thing to notice or suggest. Yet there are at least two unlikely exceptions to this phenomenon: mainstream rap music and mainstream stand-up comedy. From the perspective of pure vulgarity, both idioms peaked around 1990.

Hip-hop acts like 2 Live Crew do not exist anymore, and they never will again. Verbally, no one will ever explore the realm of uncharted tastelessness with such limitless ambition (other artists could go *as far,* but they can't go further, unless we invent some totally new words for the vagina). The same can be said for comedian Andrew Dice Clay. This is because a) they worked within a language-based medium, and b) we have a finite amount of usable profanity. Both 2 Live Crew and Andrew Dice Clay reduced their respective art forms down to literal nursery rhymes, completely devoid of (what we normally describe as) creativity. 2 Live Crew wrote songs like "Fuck Shop" (where *fuck* is used twenty-two times in less than three and a half minutes) and "Face Down, Ass Up" (self-explanatory). Their album *As Nasty as They Wanna Be* sold far beyond expectations (particularly among suburban audiences) and was, of course, controversial in its time: It's now possible to visit the Rock and Roll Hall of Fame and examine the court documents from their 1990 obscenity case in Florida's Broward County (the album was initially deemed obscene, but that ruling was overturned on appeal). Three decades later, 2 Live Crew no longer seems unsettling; somehow, songs like "Me So Horny" are now goofy and delightful. Almost no one views 2 Live Crew's music as *important,* but only the most puritan consider it *problematic.* Luther Campbell doesn't seem that far removed from "Weird Al" Yankovic. "Me So Horny" is sick and raw, but it's also cute. It's funny that someone decided that this was a good way to make music. It's funny that it happened at all.

Yet this is not how history views Andrew Dice Clay.

People loved him in 1990 and people hated him in 1990. Now they only hate him (not as intensely, but more homogeneously). His signature routines do not seem charming in retrospect. They just seem mean-spirited, and not even particularly daring. They seem worse now than they did back then, which is the opposite of how this is supposed to work.

This is how it's supposed to work: An uncompromising comedian goes further than society is comfortable with and pays a price in the present-tense. He (or she) draws attention, but most of that attention is negative. He is labeled as polarizing. The ensuing controversy causes the size of his audience to spike . . . but that brand of ephemeral popularity fades just as fast. The comedian starts to seem like a caricature and provisionally disappears. But then—years later, and especially if he dies—that same comedian is rediscovered as a universal genius. People change their own memory of who the person was and how they once felt about his persona. The artist becomes less defined by the specificity of his material and more defined by the unspecific idea of what his comedy was supposed to achieve. Over time, the fact that he went "too far" is precisely what makes him beloved. Obvious examples of this transition involve Lenny Bruce, Bill Hicks, Andy Kaufman, and Richard Pryor; smaller-scale versions have happened to Don Rickles, Joan Rivers, Redd Foxx, and Larry David. It will happen to Gilbert Gottfried within the next ten years. And it seems like it should have already happened to Andrew Dice Clay. It seems like he was genetically engineered to have that kind of comeback. But he won't. The pendulum is not swinging back. He will always be vilified, and dying won't help. The fact that he resurfaced in a recurring role in the final season of *Entourage* actually made things worse, because the qualities people don't like about Clay perfectly dovetailed with all the qualities they don't like about *Entourage*. Being on *Entourage* actively reminded people that they didn't like him (or that if they *did* like him, they weren't supposed to).

Now, is this the Diceman's fault? Partially. He is one-third responsible for why this happened. But there were two other factors that were beyond his control—the era of his success and the type of person who paid to see him perform. It was a perfect storm for eternal antipathy.

Let's start with the stuff that was his own fault. Clay's material was not that funny. It did not mine a deeper concept or change how people saw reality, unless you count the guys in the UK dance band EMF. But this is a minor failure; there have been many allegedly brilliant comics whose core material, and particularly their earliest attempts at stand-up, do not withstand the test of time. If you transcribed their jokes on paper, you might not even know that they were attempts at comedy. But that shortcoming can be totally overcome by character, and Clay had a strong, recognizable character. The way he talked (and the way he smoked cigarettes) was 50 percent of the act. It might have been 80 percent of the act. If you want to argue that Clay's execution was certifiably genius, that's an argument that can be made. But this was still a problem. He started his career as an impersonator (first as John Travolta, then as Jerry Lewis), and he always claims that the Diceman was an invented character. He was openly suggesting it was a character at the height of his fame. But the fact that he asserted this distance made things worse: His real personality seemed unnecessarily close to the fake character he claimed to be manufacturing. He wasn't totally invested in that character (like Kaufman), nor was he irrefutably pretending (like Stephen Colbert). If he had taken the former route, people would have said, "This routine is disturbing, but at least it's real." If he'd taken the latter route, he would have been seen as a satirist commenting on the entrenched hypocrisies of human sexuality. But Dice ended up splitting the difference, and that never works over the long haul. He was generating a persona that seemed exactly like the person he actually was, but still arguing that the Real Andrew Clay Silverstein was somehow separate (and that *he* could always tell the difference, even when no one else could). It was like he was choosing to become the worst idealized version of himself, without taking responsibility for what that implied. As such, he'll never get credit for being dangerously authentic or secretly insightful. The only positive memory of his career is that he was popular.

And he *was* popular. He was popular in a way that no comedian had ever been before; while other major comics had managed to sell albums, Dice could play Zeppelin-size arenas. He could sell out Madison Square Garden two nights in a row. He could sell out the 18,000-seat Nassau Coliseum in minutes. And as his career amplified, a pattern emerged: Before any massive event, there would be a profile of Clay in the local newspaper. If that media outlet managed to interview him, the angle of the feature would typically focus on the possibility that the Diceman was secretly sensitive; if he didn't grant an interview, the piece would generally focus on his critics and the magnitude of his success. Following the performance, Clay's act would inevitably be reviewed by the same publication, almost always negatively. And then the newspaper would run predictable letters from people who either loved or hated him, such as these from *Newsday* in November of 1990:

> I take strong exception to [*Newsday* writer] Paul Vitello's characterization of the fans of Andrew Dice Clay as a riotous, womanizing rabble. . . . What Vitello fails to realize is that Dice is creating a parody of a certain type of male and mocking the behavior of the females who associate with that type. Dice does not degrade women in general. . . .
>
> What disturbs me most, however, is this double standard that is employed in defining "hate comedy." Apparently, Clay's critics are not bothered by the many comics who degrade Christian Fundamentalists, anti-abortion activists and others on the political right. But when Dice mocks certain women, minorities, the handicapped, etc., this is branded as "hate comedy." . . .
>
> What we need to do is recognize comedy as such and not take it too seriously.
>
> —J.M., Wading River

Unfortunately, Paul Vitello's column on Andrew Dice Clay does not go far enough. Clay is a dangerous man. He espouses attitudes that may lead to abusive behavior in some people. Clay calls women "pigs" and "whores" and says how a man should humiliate women in public. These are the kinds of attitudes that lead directly to domestic violence and sexual harassment. In fact, I think Clay is really raping women figuratively in his act. . . .

I'd like to see Clay 40 years from now. Let's see if he finds his own act so amusing then. I find the reaction of Clay's audience most despicable. When they stand up and cheer at every remark Clay makes, the audience seems to be saying, "We love your swill! Give us more to rot our brains!"

The fact that we need a comedian like Clay tells us something is fundamentally wrong with our society. . . .

—G.S., Long Beach

In short, what we have is a popular, polarizing comedian that audiences took personally. His fans saw him as culturally necessary while his detractors exaggerated his impact. He was banned from MTV. A cast member on *Saturday Night Live* (Nora Dunn) refused to appear on the *SNL* episode he hosted, and that evening's musical guest (the equally controversial Sinead O'Connor) did the same. How you felt about Clay symbolized something about how you viewed the world. As a result, it seems as if he should be a meaningful figure to pop historians. It seems like even people who hated his material should now like the *idea* of Andrew Dice Clay, because he represented so many fascinating things. But this is not the case. Clay remains vilified, twenty years after his fame. And I suspect the reason why is the same reason the apex of his popularity was so much greater than logic dictates: It happened in 1990.

This is the part that's not his fault.

* * *

There are things we cannot control about ourselves. One of these things is the degree to which we find something to be funny. It's not a choice; our body physically reacts to the sensation of amusement. And if something feels undeniably funny—if you hear a joke and find yourself unable to keep from laughing at its content—there's no way you can view that joke as personally offensive. No one has ever honestly said, "I hate that this joke exists, even though it's clearly hilarious." It doesn't matter how controversial the topic is or what language you use. You might recognize how it could be offensive to someone else, but it can't offend you personally (if it did, you wouldn't be able to laugh). You may think that the sentiment is wrong, but it can't *feel* unfunny. This is why a handful of exceptionally transformative comedians—Louis C.K. being the current example—are allowed to talk about anything they want in a public setting: If people can't renounce their own outward amusement, they can't simultaneously claim to be hurt.

This is the standard for what's acceptable to joke about in public.

This is a totally illogical standard.

When people want to criticize a surface-level comedian, like Andrew Dice Clay (or Seth MacFarlane, or Katt Williams, or Daniel Tosh), they inevitably work from the stance that what the comedian said is "just not funny." That's always part of the argument. But what this actually means is that the comedian is not funny *enough*. What they're really talking about is the skill level of the person delivering the material and whatever they assume his (or her) motive must be. And that's flat-out idiotic. The standard should be this: If the message a comedian expresses (within the proper setting for comedy) would not be funny to any objective person, *regardless of who said it or how it was said,* then those words are unacceptable. Otherwise, it should just be considered what it is—unorthodox discourse of undefined value.

★ ★ ★

I'm reticent to use the term "political correctness." I realize it drives certain people really, really crazy. [My wife is one of these people.] However, there isn't a better term to connote the primary linguistic issue in America from (roughly) 1986 to 1995. Today, the phrase "political correctness" is mostly used as a quaint distraction. No one takes it too seriously. It feels like something that only matters to Charles Krauthammer. But in 1990, that argument was real. If you cared about ideas, you had to deal with it. At the debate's core, a meaningful philosophical question was exposed and dissected: If someone is personally offended by a specific act, does that alone qualify the act as *collectively* offensive? It's a problem that's essentially unsolvable. But what made things so insane in 1990 was the degree to which people worried about how this question would change everything about society. Up until the mid-eighties, there was always a shared assumption that the Right controlled the currency of outrage; part of what made conservatives "conservative" was their discomfort with profanity and indecency and Elvis Presley's hips. But then—somewhat swiftly, and somehow academically—it felt as if the Left was suddenly dictating what was acceptable to be infuriated over (and always for ideological motives, which is why the modifier "politically" felt essential). This created a lot of low-level anxiety whenever people argued in public. Every casual conversation suddenly had the potential to get someone fired. It was a great era for white people hoping to feel less racist by accusing other white people of being very, very racist. A piece of art could be classified as sexist simply because it *ignored* the concept of sexism. Any intended message mattered less than the received message, and every received message could be interpreted in whatever way the receiver wanted. So this became a problem for everybody. It was painlessly oppressive, and the backlash was stupid and adversarial. It drove artists to linguistic extremes, and it drove audiences to Andrew Dice Clay. He would not have been a megastar in any other historical window—it had to happen at a time when vulgarity somehow felt important.

Here is what Clay would do when he performed: He'd walk on stage, mock angry, wearing a leather jacket. He'd light a cigarette and wordlessly smoke it; this might go on for more than a minute. When he'd finally start talking, the routine would go like this . . .

DICE: Jack and Jill went up the hill, each with a buck and a
    quarter. (*pause*) Jill came down with $2.50. Ohhh!
AUDIENCE: (*together*) What a whore!

My reason for transcribing this dialogue is not to mock how unfunny it is, even though it (obviously) doesn't seem funny in the pages of a book. You can still make multiple arguments for why this material matters. For one thing, it's pretty weird (which is reason enough to care). If you're a folklorist, you might appreciate the idea of a joke based on oral tradition. If you're a sociologist, perhaps you're intrigued by the call-and-response role played by the audience (i.e., the way they would memorize all of Clay's jokes beforehand in order to shout the punchlines back at him). If you're into Freud, maybe you think sexualizing a nursery rhyme gets to the core of why it exists. But all that stuff is tangential. It's not important. What mattered was that this joke was not cognizant (or even interested) in any social mores. The only arbitrator was Clay. When the audience chimed in with "What a whore!" they were able to say something without really saying it (because they were technically speaking *for Clay,* who was latently speaking *for them*). The specific content was irrelevant as long as it was profane and unsanitized. When Andrew Dice Clay played Madison Square Garden, it became a "safe place" for twenty thousand people who wanted to feel like language was limitless and unalienable. When they laughed at the idea of calling a homosexual a "cocksucker," it was partially because they were homophobic and thought it was funny . . . but it was also because they knew this sentiment would disgust a certain type of self-righteous person protesting outside the venue's walls. Dice's fans felt like they were hearing something more real than what was happening in an increasingly artificial society. They saw it as straightforward and self-evident: Homosexual men *do* perform oral sex on other men, men *do* refer to their penis as a cock, and performing oral sex *does require* said cock to be sucked. In the minds of his supporters, Clay was hated for describing the world as it actually was. That was always the best pro-Dice argument—the world was becoming too sensitive, so he was forced to serve as the charmless counterbalance. And some people loved him for that. They loved that he would happily allow himself to be demonized. To those who thought political correctness was ruining America, he was a soldier they'd pay twenty-five dollars to see, just to hear him say "cunt" in public without fear or empathy.

But these people lost the war. And while all those ticket-buying bystanders could just move on and pretend they were never there, the Diceman would nay recover. He was a casualty, and his injuries were mortal.

It was a war of attrition. The winners didn't make a better argument, but they wore the culture down. [Here, again, we see the inevitable: Over time, the winners are always the progressives.] Almost everything that advocates of the speech-limitation movement wanted in 1990 have been adopted by the world at large; in virtually all situations, we err on the side of the potentially offended (this, more than anything else, is the best argument *against* the idea of an ever-coarsening culture). In 2012, the most talked-about piece of entertainment was the HBO show *Girls,* a high-end sitcom about four twenty-something women living in New York. Its second episode made jokes about abortion and date rape, but that wasn't what made it problematic; what bothered people was the fact that all four of the main characters were affluent and Caucasian. Because the show felt generationally significant, a seemingly endless stream of writers complained that its unwillingness to reflect every kind of person living in Brooklyn made the essence of *Girls* slightly racist. For two bizarre weeks in April, there were insular media debates about the insidious danger of "ironic racism." This prompted one of the writers on *Girls* (Lesley Arfin) to sarcastically Tweet the following: "What really bothered me most about [the movie] *Precious* was that there was no representation of ME." Considering how the other omnipresent criticism of *Girls* was its self-conscious narcissism, this was pretty clever (and grounded in reality, since the concept of any fictional creation equally representing all manifestations of diversity is both irrational and impossible). But Arfin had to retract her quip, and *The New Yorker* deemed her "breathtakingly dismissive and intellectually dishonest." This reaction surprised no one, including those who did not find her Tweet remotely troubling. I'm sure Arfin wasn't surprised, since (I assume) she courted this negative attention on purpose. Every savvy person now accepts that uncomfortable ideas can't be expressed in public without some consideration for how various levels of ideologue will misinterpret the message. Self-editing is far more important than creativity (and only Quentin Tarantino appears immune). If you want to experience a free-flowing discourse devoid of limitation, you need to seek the darkest fringes of the Internet (and none of that anonymous bile can bleed back into proper society, because the interpretation always ends up being worse than the original sentiment). As a whole, this has been a net positive for America. It had to happen. Modern people have been raised to personalize everything they encounter and absorb, even when it has nothing to do with their own life experience. I used to feel far differently about such realities; as a twenty-year-old, I was a full-on First Amendment fascist. I saw every possible conflict as a free speech issue: stand-up comedy, "Cop Killer," the use of Native American nicknames by collegiate sports teams, local noise ordinances, seat belt laws, perjury, and the legal definition of "all the shrimp you can eat." I was the Patrick Henry of Ponderosa Steakhouse. But I've mellowed over time, which is what all wine drunks and dope smokers say when trying to justify why they quit trying. The Constitution is awesome, but still overrated; it's like *Pet Sounds*. The wide-scale adoption of political correctness was silly, but not unreasonable. The freedom that was lost was mostly theoretical and rarely necessary. No one is significantly worse off.

Except, I suppose, Andrew Dice Clay.

This, I must concede, is not exactly a tragedy. It doesn't make me sad that Clay has not been rediscovered as some kind of game-changing genius, and I don't think he necessarily deserves to have that happen (he can have a one-hour special on Showtime, but that's probably enough). If we're going to classify certain celebrities as *villains* based on the actual content of their art, the Diceman's stand-up routine warrants inclusion. It was degrading and it was repetitive. But we all know that's not how it works. Merit is always a factor in someone's cultural memory, but rarely the main one. I can easily imagine many alternative scenarios where Andrew Clay is a beloved figure: if he'd had less commercial success; if his only known recording was *The Day the Laughter Died*; if Woody Allen had put him in a movie in 1983 instead of 2013; if he hadn't embraced the sector of his fan base who refused to see him as a satirist. Any one of those hypotheticals might have reversed everything. But Dice had the wrong fans at the right time. He was mostly himself, but not totally. Somebody had to pay for how the world had changed.

WITHOUT A GUN
THEY CAN'T GET NONE

Chuck D gets involved in all that black stuff. We don't.
Fuck that black power shit: We don't give a fuck. Free
South Africa? We don't give a fuck. I bet there ain't
anybody in South Africa wearing a button saying "Free
Compton" or "Free California." They don't give a
damn about us, so why should we give a damn about
them? We're not into politics at all. N.W.A is just saying what other people are afraid to say.

> —Ice Cube, talking about his life
> as if it were a movie.

Don't get a movie confused with real life. I'm a well-
rounded human being like everyone else.

> —Ice Cube, talking about a movie
> as if it were his life.

If someone pretends to be nice (and if we *know* they're pretending,
either by their own admission or from past experience), we pretend
not to give that person credit as a humanitarian. Such behavior is
considered phony, and those who use niceness as currency are
categorized as insincere. But this logic only applies in a vacuum, or

in those rare real-life moments that have a vacuum-packed flavor. For the most part, holding people to this standard is an impossible way to exist. Most of what we classify as "niceness" is effortlessly fake. When I walk into a convenience store and give the kid behind the counter two dollars for a $1.50 bottle of Gatorade, I say thanks when he gives me my change. But what am I thankful for? He's just doing his job, and the money he returns is mine. The kid behind the counter likewise says thanks to me, but I have done nothing to warrant his gratitude; I wanted something in the store and paid him exactly what it cost. It's not like he brewed the Gatorade or invented the brand. I didn't select his particular store for any reason beyond proximity, and he doesn't own the building or the franchise. From either perspective, the relationship is no different from that of a human and a vending machine. We only say "thank you" to be seen as nice. We secretly know that being seen as nice is the same as being nice in actuality. If you present yourself as a nice person, that becomes the prism for how your other actions are judged. The deeper motives that drive you can only be questioned by those who know you exceptionally well, and (most of the time) not even by them. If you act nice, you're nice. That's the whole equation. Nobody cares *why* you say thank you. Nobody is *supposed* to care; weirdly, this is something we're never supposed to question. It's impractical to incessantly interrogate the veracity of every stranger who seems like a blandly nice citizen. It's rude. Until proven otherwise, we just accept goodness at face value.

But this is not how it works with badness.

If someone *wants* to be perceived as a bad person, it's immediately assumed to have a wider ulterior purpose. Decency is its own reward, but purposeful depravity requires an upside. Moreover, the authenticity of every self-constructed villain is always up for debate, particularly when their specific brand of villainy represents the bedrock of their identity; since we assume normal people would always prefer to be seen as good, those who seem proud of their badness are immediately suspect. They come across as contrived, and that bothers people more than whatever wickedness they assert. It's a circular construction that sustains the intended reality: We question the sincerity of the man who wants to be evil, because the man who desires evil is almost certainly a liar (which validates his claim, because liars are evil). So perhaps badness is a little like goodness, at least in this one respect. Wanting it is enough to make it real.

No major musical group put more effort into being vilified than the members of N.W.A. No one else comes close, really; all the other examples fall too short or go too far (and thus drift into caricature). It's like they wrote the villainy handbook, or at least stole the handbook and used it as a design for life. On their debut album, *Straight Outta Compton,* they directly use the word *villain* a repetitive thirteen times, although that's partially because it was the nickname for one of their members.

[Another (less symbolic) reason for the overabundant use of the word *villain* in hip-hop is because it so nicely rhymes with the words *chillin'* and *illin'.* It's the same reason pop-metal bands often find ways to use "action" and "satisfaction" within the same verse.]

When deployed in rap vernacular, the word *villain* feels slightly anachronistic, particularly when prefaced by the adjective *motherfuckin'.* It's a little old-timey. But there simply wasn't a word that better described N.W.A's public aspirations with such accuracy. I suppose *gangsta* is the only other word that came close, a modifier so flexible it could even be used to describe how rappers operated their cars. If you lowered the seat and tilted your body toward the vehicle's passenger side, the posture was referred to as the "gangsta lean." Spawned in 1972 by forgotten R&B wunderkind William DeVaughn, "gangsta lean" is an amazingly evocative term, particularly to those who did not initially know what it meant. But once you unpacked the definition, it merely outlined a villainous way to drive your jalopy to White Castle, operating from the position that appearing villainous was an important way to appear at all possible times. This was very, very important to the members of N.W.A. It was the only thing they seemed to worry about. Everything they attempted had to possess criminal undertones. I can only assume they spent hours trying to deduce villainous ways to microwave popcorn (and if they'd succeeded, there would absolutely be a song about it, assumedly titled "Pop Goes the Corn Killa" or "45 Seconds to Bitch Snack").

Straight Outta Compton was released in 1988. Its cultural apex in America was 1989. I lived in North Dakota, so I never heard it until 1991 (around the same time Axl Rose was wearing an N.W.A hat in the "You Could Be Mine" video). The first person who played it for me was a Native American medical student, the closest thing to a black guy in my wing of the dormitory. When I asked him who it was, he said the full name as three one-word sentences. *"Niggers. With. Attitude."* This, I immediately told him, was not correct. Though I'd never heard their music, I'd read about N.W.A in various magazines. I informed him that "Niggers" was actually pronounced "Niggaz" and that "with" was actually "wit" and that "Attitude" was supposed to be pluralized (although I can't say he was really wrong about that last part, since the entire group seemed to share the same singular attitude about everything). I think his response to my correction was something along the lines of, "Well, good for you." His next sentence was, "So what do you think of this fucking record?"

Obviously, I can't jump back into my body and totally relive the experience of hearing those songs for the first time. I wish I could. But my memory is that it followed this approximate trajectory, sequenced in five-minute intervals:

1) "This sounds awesome."
2) "Hmm. Actually, this is more disturbing than I expected."
3) "This seems wrong to me. These ideas are bad for society."

4) "Wait—these dudes are into Steve Miller?"
5) "Hmm. Perhaps this is important. Perhaps I should write about this for my Psychology of Communication class."
6) "Is this even real? Because it sure does sound awesome."

Now, on the day I first listened to *Straight Outta Compton,* I'd (critically) listened to only two other hip-hop albums: Public Enemy's *It Takes a Nation of Millions to Hold Us Back* (on the advisement of *Rolling Stone* magazine) and Public Enemy's *Fear of a Black Planet* (based on the advisement of the group itself). I could not physically locate *Yo! Bum Rush the Show* anywhere in Fargo. [For whatever reason, I did not count the Beastie Boys, Tone Lōc's *Lōc'ed After Dark,* or my mostly ignored copy of *He's the DJ, I'm the Rapper* as authentic rap; I unconsciously viewed these albums as Rap For White People, which my 1991 self viewed as "regular music."] As a result, my collegiate perception of hip-hop was completely based on a two-artist continuum (Public Enemy on the left, N.W.A on the right). To me, PE was musical, smart, and impractical. They were outraged by historical problems that seemed impossible to verify, such as whoever killed Malcolm X and the culpability of the Jews in Christ's crucifixion. It felt like *art,* or at least like people trying to be artful. I did not feel this way about N.W.A. They seemed way less complex, but that was because it was so easy to comprehend the lyrics on the very first listen. There was something untethered about the sonic velocity (Greil Marcus once joked that Robert Johnson would have been the producer of *Straight Outta Compton* had he somehow lived to the age of one hundred). I assumed the guys in N.W.A were crazy, and—at least in my unknowingly racist mind—*accidentally* smart, as if I was somehow inferring complex things that they were not intentionally implying. My deepest connection came during "Fuck tha Police," where Ice Cube outlined a specific type of police confrontation I had never previously considered:

And on the other hand, without a gun they can't get none
But don't let it be a black and a white one
'cause they'll slam ya down to the street top
Black police showin' out for the white cop

The idea of a black policeman abusing a black citizen in order to impress his white coworker obliterated my nineteen-year-old mind. And if it had come off *Fear of a Black Planet,* I'm sure I would have thought, "Well, this is their intention. This group is educational. They are telling me about interesting theoretical possibilities that I need to consider when thinking about the world." But that's not what I thought when I heard it from N.W.A. Instead I thought, "Wow. That must happen all the time." And this wasn't because I trusted Ice Cube more than Chuck D, because I generally trusted him less; it was because N.W.A seemed totally devoid of a social agenda. Things just meant what they meant. If they wanted to express something, they simply said the words (seemingly without consideration for how those words might be received or misinterpreted). There were lots of contradictions, and I liked contradictions. For example: The line everyone remembers from *Straight Outta Compton* is Cube's defining mantra, "Life ain't nuthin' but bitches and money." It embodied the ethos of the entire genre, and—over time—I've heard it sardonically applied to just about every possible situation life can offer. Yet elsewhere on the very same record, Eazy-E asks, "So what about the bitch who got shot? Fuck her! You think I give a damn about a bitch? I ain't a sucker." In other words, life is only about bitches and money, but even the bitches don't particularly matter. This is weapon-grade nihilism: There were only two meaningful elements within their entire worldview . . . and one could be totally eliminated without consequence!

When pressed by the media (and in the rare instances when they took that media seriously), the guys in N.W.A deferred to "reality" (always the best available argument in any situation where no logical argument exists). They referred to their music as "reality rap" and argued that critics of *Straight Outta Compton* were simply afraid of what its overwhelming realness reflected about the condition of America. "Most people in Compton don't give a fuck," reiterated Eazy. "All we do is rap about it." Years later, I would come to realize that N.W.A's portrait of reality was not believed by anyone who took their music as seriously as it deserved, regardless of how they felt about it aesthetically. But the cumulative weight of that disbelief had the desired effect. It performed better than reality.

The original lineup of N.W.A was composed of six members, but the meaningful lineup was only five: Ice Cube, Eazy-E, Dr. Dre, MC Ren (aka the Ruthless Villain), and DJ Yella. [The group's extraneous sixth member, Arabian Prince, exited before they became famous.] They were all different people, but they dressed like clones: They wore black jackets and black hats promoting the Los Angeles Kings and the Los Angeles Raiders. By chance, N.W.A's rise to power occurred during a strange period when hockey was extremely popular in L.A. (due to Wayne Gretzky's 1988 arrival from Edmonton) and the awkward twelve-year stretch when the Raiders left Oakland to play football in the Los Angeles Coliseum. The Kings and the Raiders both wore black and silver. The Kings—who'd previously dressed in gold and purple, like the Lakers—started wearing black and silver in '88 because they wanted to be more like the Raiders. It was the same thing N.W.A wanted.

Anyone who wants to be bad on purpose wants to be like the Raiders.

The Raiders are an anomaly in pro sports, comparable with no other professional sports organization in America. Regardless of their geographic location or the components of their roster, the franchise has sustained the same philosophical template for almost fifty years. This is especially rare when one considers how often sports franchises have no philosophical template at all.

There are certain principles the Raiders have always followed, even during periods when doing so worked against them. These principles are:

1) **Draft for speed.** This is why—in 2009—the Raiders selected little-known Maryland receiver Darrius Heyward-Bey in the first round of the draft. He had the fastest forty-yard-dash time at the NFL combine. It is the franchise belief that speed can be acquired, but not taught. Bey was supposed to be the modern version of Cliff Branch, the Raiders' deep threat throughout the 1970s. The Raiders incessantly aspire to replicate their own past.

2) **Combine a power running game with a vertical, downfield passing attack.** This is the logical extension of the first principle. The Raiders' long-standing offensive approach has been to pound teams on the ground and then burn them deep. They've always overvalued strong-armed quarterbacks who take downfield risks, starting with Daryle Lamonica in 1967. A notable exception to this strategy was the brief coaching tenure of Jon Gruden from 1998 to 2001, when the Raiders ran a West Coast system that emphasized short, ball-controlled passing. This was also the last time the Raiders played in a Super Bowl.

3) **Reward excessively physical play, even when it results in unnecessary penalties. Consider those penalties the price of doing business.** In 2011, Oakland set the NFL record for the most penalties in a season. But that record is merely one spike in their overall history: The Raiders have always been among the most penalized teams in football (they've led the NFL in that category fourteen times), with particular dominance in the idiom of severe 15-yard unsportsmanlike penalties.

4) **Sign players that other teams are unwilling to accept.**
This is essential.
5) **Never police problematic off-the-field behavior.** In fact,
celebrate that behavior.
6) **"Just win, baby."**

The first two principles apply to how the game is played on the field, so their meaning is mostly technical. The third principle toggles between how the game is played and how the game is perceived, so it has symbolic import. But it's those final three principles that matter most. They are purely ideological. They represent the ethos of the Raider organization, and they're the worldview of one man: Al Davis. When you think about the Raiders in the abstract, he is the only person who needs to be considered in the concrete. In 1962, he was named the Raiders' head coach and general manager; by 1976, he was the team's principal owner and the architect behind every move it made (a position he inflexibly retained until his death from heart failure in 2011). The only reason the Raiders managed to sustain one model for five decades is that they were completely controlled by one personality for that entire period. This will never happen again. He was the last dragon. When writing about football (or any sport), a phrase that's often thrown around is "the modern era." In pro football, it's customary to claim that the modern era starts with the inception of the Super Bowl, or the 1970 merger of the NFL and the AFL, or the '78 rule changes that accelerated the passing game. But this is only because we never think of history having a future. When NFL historians debate this question in a hundred years, the clever ones will suggest that the league's modern era didn't start until the day after Al Davis died. He was the end of the beginning. We're only crawling out of the Precambrian now.

For the sake of transparency, I should probably mention that Al Davis is (pretty much) my favorite sports owner of all time. For the sake of balance, I should also note that he was an awful person who openly encouraged cheating. He's my favorite, but not because I like him. In the wake of his death, some of his more reprehensible acts now seem charming (throughout the sixties, rival coaches believed he planted secret microphones in his opponents' locker room). Yet so much of what he did was simply mean-spirited. He enjoyed being hated, or at least he didn't mind. In 1992, future Hall of Fame running back Marcus Allen gave an interview on ABC in which he claimed that Davis was trying to end his career and wreck his livelihood, even though Allen had been the Raiders' MVP in Super Bowl XVIII. Davis seemed self-destructive in counterintuitive ways; he often behaved as if his interior goal was to wreck the NFL (he sued the league three times and even sided with the upstart USFL in an ill-fated 1986 antitrust suit). His iconic phrase, "Just win, baby," might sound like an innocuous rah-rah motto, but there was something perverse about his insertion of the word *just*. When combined with the persona Al Davis fostered (and particularly when the phrase oozed from Al's own larynx), that extraneous *just* seemed like the amoral justification for everything he did. He wanted the world to view him as totally ruthless, a quality he associated with power. Davis was a civil rights activist and a rare pro-labor owner, but these qualities are not what people remember. What people remember is that Al Davis was a Jew who openly expressed a fascination with Adolf Hitler. Think about that: It wasn't just that he was a Jew with a weird, unspoken attraction to Hitler's role in world history; he was a Jew *who wanted people to know* that he thought Hitler was super interesting.

He loved the contradiction. He loved how it bothered people. It was an advantage.

"For a long time I thought I was a Jew and I was happy to be a Jew," Danish director Lars von Trier said at a Cannes Film Festival press conference, promoting his 2011 film *Melancholia*. He was sitting next to Kirsten Dunst, who periodically gasped as his extemporaneous dialogue continued. "But it turned out that I was not a Jew, and even if I'd been a Jew, I would have been a second-rate Jew, because there's a kind of hierarchy in the Jewish population. But, anyway, I really wanted to be a Jew, and then I found out I'm really a Nazi, because my family was German, which also gave me some kind of pleasure. What can I say? I understand Hitler. But I think he did some wrong things, yes, absolutely, but I can see him sitting in his bunker in the end . . . I think I understand the man. He's not what you would call a good guy, but I understand much about him, and I sympathize with him a little bit, yes. But come on, I'm not for the Second World War."

It will come as little surprise that these words got von Trier banned from a festival that was actively celebrating his work. He initially apologized, but then retracted his apology in *GQ*, essentially arguing that to apologize for what he considered a joke would be akin to apologizing for who he was as a human. Considered rationally, it's obvious von Trier should never have apologized at all. Von Trier did not say he *liked* Hitler; he said he *understood* Hitler (which, as a director, is what he's supposed to do—he's supposed to place himself inside the perspective of abnormal viewpoints). But the main reason he shouldn't have apologized was because he was never sorry. He was joking, fully aware that what he said would not be taken as a joke. His goal was to make a certain kind of person hate him (and by "certain kind," I do not mean Jewish people—I mean the type of people who actively enjoy the sensation of outrage, Jewish or otherwise). "He spoke with grotesque insensitivity; he acted like a jerk," moaned *The New Yorker*, seemingly unaware that this was his objective. For his art to succeed, Lars von Trier needs to be despised by the reactionary segment of his liberal audience. His movies aim to confront people with ideas they will never truly accept: *Melancholia* is about how the end of the world might be positive. *Dogville* is about the inherent evil of the American experiment; its quasi-sequel,

Manderlay, implies that racism is both inevitable and unconquer-able. *The Idiots* suggests humans are irrevocably trapped by their own inhibitions. *Dancer in the Dark* is about how Björk was such an ineffective factory employee she had to be executed (or some-thing along those lines—I didn't totally get that one).

Like the '88 version of Eazy-E, von Trier is a performative nihilist. We never know how he really feels about anything, but his public posture is to the left of morality. His films are so deft and disturbing and antihuman that it's easy to perceive them as satire, which is what some audiences prefer to do; because his films are a rare example of high-art explorations within a mostly middlebrow medium, middlebrow critics *want* to like them. They want to be intellectually associated with an auteur who makes great movies, so they're tempted to reframe his work as some-thing postmodern. They want him to be an ironist. But von Trier realizes that his movies are important only if taken at face value. They can't have malleable interpretations. They need to be expe-rienced from the standpoint that he really does believe the end of the world might be a great thing, because that's what pushes a project like *Melancholia* outside the realm of conventional cinema. You need to view von Trier as a talented, terrible person. He has to wear the black hat, and no hat is blacker than the one resting upon the brain that relates to Hitler.

N.W.A wore Raiders gear because of what the Raiders represent (and because they were local), but also because the Raiders hap-pen to wear black. Sometimes things are simple. But here is some-thing less simple: In 1988, Mark G. Frank and Thomas Gilovich of Cornell University published a study titled "The Dark Side of Self-and Social Perception: Black Uniforms and Aggression in Profes-sional Sports." It starts from the premise that black connotes evil and death in all cultures and hopes to figure out if "these associa-tions influence people's behavior in important ways. For example, does wearing black clothing lead both the wearer and others to

perceive him or her as more evil and aggressive? More impor-
tantly, does it lead the wearer to actually *act* more aggressive?"
It will probably not surprise you that their ultimate supposition
is yes. (I can't imagine anyone would know this study even exists
if the answer had been no.) One of the metrics the researchers
invent is something they call the "Malevolence Rating." Twenty-
five random people (none of whom followed sports) were each
paid two dollars to look at various NFL and NHL uniforms and
rank them on various continuums (good/bad, nice/mean, timid/
aggressive). The study's conclusion is that the Raiders have the
most malevolent overall appearance (the Miami Dolphins are
seen as the least malevolent, which suggests Axl Rose might have
been one of the twenty-five people polled). I will grant that this is
a questionable way to validate a theory that already seems intuitively true. But what's harder to prove is the second part of the
question, and that's the question that matters: What makes the
Raiders act the way they do? Is it conscious or unconscious?

There are two Raiders who best represent the ambiguity of this
problem: Jack Tatum and John Matuszak. Both are now deceased.
Tatum was among the best defensive backs of the 1970s and is
widely viewed as the hardest-hitting free safety of his era. Nick-
named the Assassin, he is best remembered for inflicting a tragedy:
In a 1978 preseason game against the New England Patriots, Tatum
paralyzed Patriot wide receiver Darryl Stingley from the chest
down. He did not intend to break the man's spine, and there was
no penalty on the play. It was a clean hit (although today he would
have been severely fined by the league office). Tatum's reputation
and livelihood was based on violence, and the hit on Stingley was
no different from what he tried to do to every opponent on every
play. But what will always be weird about this event was Tatum's
reaction. He supposedly tried to visit Stingley in the hospital, but
found himself unwelcome by the immediate family; as a result, the
two men never spoke, ever. Tatum never apologized. "It's about
who can hit the hardest," he said in 2007, the week of Stingley's

ultimate death. "That's what the game is about." There are those who insist Tatum was privately troubled by what happened, but there's a lot of public evidence that suggests otherwise—most notably, Tatum's three ridiculously titled autobiographies: *They Call Me Assassin* (1980), *They Still Call Me Assassin* (1989), and *Final Confessions of NFL Assassin Jack Tatum* (1996). Why would a player who put a man in a wheelchair (during an exhibition game!) have such an unquenchable desire to be identified as a killing machine? Only a player who sees that designation as central to who he is. Tatum is the argument for consciousness: He wanted to be vilified by others because that is how he viewed himself.

The situation with Matuszak is less clear-cut. The first overall pick of the 1973 draft, he was a powerful but generally under-achieving defensive end. He was far more dangerous off the field. Matuszak was a six-foot-eight, 280-pound cocaine addict who owned a lot of guns and once ended up in a straitjacket (report-edly due to an overdose of booze and barbiturates). He claimed to consume Valium and vodka for breakfast and was charged with four DUIs. In 1986, he was unsuccessfully sued by a male stripper who claimed Matuszak threw him across a bar. Yet there was something peculiar about the way Matuszak viewed his own character: He always talked like a smart person pretending to be dumb, except when he acted like a dumb person pretending to be smart.

"When you say I epitomize the Raiders," Matuszak once told a broadcaster, "and then you say the Raiders aren't very well liked, I guess what you're trying to say is that the Raid-ers—as well as John Matuszak—have always been . . . *contro-versial*." In Matuszak's defense, he seemed a little high when he said that. But this is the kind of attitude that made him confus-ing; he seemed unhappy that he was self-aware. What Matuszak really wanted to say in that interview was that anyone who sug-gested he epitomized the Raiders was fundamentally suggesting that he was a legalized criminal (and that this was undeniably true). He knew it, but he saw it as something partially outside of himself. He wrote about this in his entertaining autobiography, *Cruisin' with the Tooz*: "When people expect you to be wild, talk about you being wild, encourage you to be wild, you begin to *be* wild. It's almost as if you *become* your image." Certainly he was not the first celebrity to claim that other people's perception of him eventually usurped his actual self. But Matuszak is an exaggerated example of this phenomenon. Before signing with Oakland, he'd struggled with Houston, Kansas City, and Washington. His limited ability as a player was not enough to mitigate his behavior as a citizen; for all those other teams, he wasn't worth the trouble. But Al Davis saw this differently. When Davis met Matuszak for the first time, the Tooz was wearing a black suit with a silver shirt; Davis immediately understood what he had. Matuszak would be a loyal monster, and his problematic personality was added value. His mere presence proved that the Raiders did not operate like other organizations (whatever he contributed on the field was pretty much gravy). Because of rogues like Matuszak, unhappy free agents gravitated to Oakland (a phenomenon that continues to this day). It became the destination franchise for every disenfranchised football player because Davis *did not require consciousness.* Playing for Al Davis meant you didn't have to accept any preexisting conditions of morality or appearance. You did not have to think about what your actions meant to the outside world. If you wanted to be a histrionic crazy-eyed killer, that was fine—but it was just as acceptable to be the complete opposite (one example was Raider tight end Dave Casper, a well-educated eccentric who preferred fishing to partying). Nothing was inflexible. The Raiders were not villains because everyone on the team was a reprobate; the Raiders were villains because everyone on the team was intellectually free. That's villainy's upside. The downside is that Matuszak died from heart failure at the age of thirty-eight and no one was remotely surprised.

* * *

Nobody believes N.W.A anymore. I'm not sure anyone completely believed them ever. When Rodney King's 1991 beating led to the 1992 L.A. riots, there was a moment when "Fuck tha Police" seemed super prescient—but that moment passed. It became a footnote. Instead, everyone returned to a more distanced interpretation of their work, a position dependent on the notion that *Straight Outta Compton* was a well-made cartoon: "*It's not about a salary / It's all about reality* they chant as they talk shit about how bad they are," Robert Christgau wrote at the time of its release. "Right, it's not about salary—it's about royalties, about brandishing scarewords like *street* and *crazy* and *fuck* and *reality* until suckers black and white cough up the cash." Still, he graded the record a B. When *Spin* published an alternative album guide in 1995, *Straight Outta Compton* scored 10 out of 10—but writer Greg Sandow still retroactively attacked their aesthetic authenticity: "We now know the group was hollow at its core—Eazy-E, who bankrolled it and promoted himself as its major star, couldn't even write his own raps."

This has become the only sophisticated way to think about N.W.A: It's essential to appreciate the concept while discounting the realism. You have to take it seriously and unseriously at the same time. For the guys in the group, it could not have worked out better. In 1989, the FBI foolishly wrote a letter condemning N.W.A. [The missive noted that seventy-eight law-enforcement officers were "feloniously slain in the line of duty during 1988 . . . and recordings such as the one from N.W.A are both discouraging and degrading to these brave, dedicated officers."] Immediately, every intellectual sided with the Compton musicians. How could the FBI believe that this album was anything except a brilliant spoof? Persecution made the group seem smarter. N.W.A's true fan base agreed with that assessment, although with fewer complications—they saw *Straight Outta Compton* as straightforward entertainment. Who even cared if it was real or fake? Wasn't the larger message of the album to not care about *anything*? "I don't give a fuck," Cube rapped relentlessly. "That's the problem." To people who valued ideas, N.W.A knew the most; to people who valued an uncompromising assault, N.W.A cared the least.

Straight Outta Compton will never disappear. It will always be the most important gangsta-rap document and the first hyper-meaningful hip-hop record to come from the West Coast. In its aftermath, N.W.A slowly collapsed in a less than electrifying manner: Ice Cube quit the group in 1989 over financial disagreements. The other members accused him of cowardice, but Cube's solo career was colossal (he's now mostly an actor, shilling for products like Coors beer and often playing the type of character he once bragged about murdering). On his 1991 album *Death Certificate,* Cube tried to revise (and reverse) the group's history with the Raiders, essentially claiming the organization had somehow ripped him off ("Stop givin' juice to the Raiders / 'cause Al Davis / never paid us"). This, however, faded with time: In 2011, Ice Cube even directed a documentary for ESPN in which he interviewed the (by then decrepit) NFL owner and treated him like a don.

After Cube's evaporation, the four remaining N.W.A members still managed a number-one album in 1991 (*Niggaz4Life*), but it lacked the incendiary insight of their previous work. Dr. Dre left the group in '91 over an ugly dispute with Eazy-E and created one of the biggest hip-hop albums of all time, *The Chronic.* Dre is now primarily focused on production and entrepreneurship, sometimes appearing in Dr Pepper commercials as himself. Eazy-E's subsequent musical career was less memorable; he died from AIDS in 1995 at the age of thirty-one, having sired at least seven kids from six different women (the real number of his offspring might be closer to twenty, but these things are hard to verify). The two less famous members, DJ Yella and MC Ren, are generally only mentioned in retrospective discussions about the heyday of N.W.A (but almost always in a complimentary manner, as is so often the case with forgotten role players). On the whole, it's impossible to view N.W.A as anything except an irrefutable success, simply because they only espoused two highly attainable goals: to make a lot of money and to not care about anything. They were bad guys on purpose, so they were able to define their own rules.

If I was reading this book, the following thought might occur to me: I might wonder if publishing a sympathetic book about villains is the author's way of actively placing himself within the villain category, which would mean the author is trying to be a villain on purpose (which is what the previous chapter was all about). I would wonder if this was some kind of attempt to write about himself through the guise of writing about other people.

At first, this would seem self-evident. But then I would think about it longer and realize the exact opposite is closer to the truth.

ARRESTED FOR SMOKING

Because so many mercantile intellectuals now write about television for a living, it's become pretty much impossible for any TV critic to express views that make straightforward sense. The volume of deep television writing is (suddenly) much too large; everything except the most unorthodox perspectives is instantly ignored. The expectation for those who cover modern television is that they will consistently interpret the experience of TV in radical, personal ways. Writers always need to be seeing something that isn't obvious (and, preferably, they need to be seeing things that serve as a parallel commentary on unrelated problems). Here's one example: Around the Presidents' Day holiday of 2012, the PBS series *American Experience* broadcast *Clinton,* a four-hour examination of the forty-second POTUS. The *New York Times* wrote about this documentary. This is how the article opened:

"Monica Lewinsky doesn't matter anymore."

One sentence. Five words, one paragraph. I was immediately intrigued. What might this mean? What was the author suggesting? It felt telling.

But then I read the next two sentences.

"It's remarkable, really, how little resonance that Clinton sex scandal has today. The White House intern who shook the world is barely ever mentioned in the 2012 presidential campaign."

What the writer was trying to do was set up her main criticism, which is that this four-hour documentary invested too much time on Bill Clinton's affair with Monica Lewinsky and failed to unpack the more meaningful political hot spots of his eight years in office. (The story's conclusion: "*Clinton* is fun to watch . . . but mostly a wasted opportunity.") I can't fault her for doing this. I did the same thing at various points in my newspaper career. Sometimes you just need to write *something* to fill a space that must be filled, and sometimes that filler makes no sense when dissected critically. This is simply another illustration of that omnipresent media problem. Because in those three sentences, the writer manages to be misleading in four different ways:

1) The Lewinsky scandal broke in 1998. In what possible framework would any political candidate (or even a political reporter) directly bring up Lewinsky's name in 2012? How would that work, exactly? In what context would it not seem specious, attacking, and unrelated to the election at hand?

2) Moreover, there are many things that don't come up in presidential elections that still remain historically important. How often do modern political candidates mention the Vietnam War?

3) *Clinton* was a comprehensive documentary. Doesn't the fact that the filmmakers themselves saw this affair (and Clinton's subsequent impeachment) as integral to his legacy serve as a significant contradiction to the premise that "Monica Lewinsky doesn't matter anymore"? She clearly mattered to the creators of this program, most of whom likely considered this problem more than anyone else.

4) Is there *anyone* who doesn't see Clinton's inability to stop himself from receiving oral sex from an intern as the most unavoidable prism through which we attempt to understand the complexity of his character (not to mention how totally fucking insane it was that this happened at all)?

Now, it's entirely possible that what the writer of this *New York Times* piece was trying to argue was that Monica Lewinsky *shouldn't* matter anymore, and maybe she thought that writing those words might somehow make them true. Certainly, there's a vague sophistication in insisting that Clinton's sexual misadventures are irrelevant to any serious discourse about political history. But that's backward. In truth, it matters way more than we like to admit (and in a hundred years, it will be the *only* thing non-historians will remember about Bill Clinton, unless his wife somehow becomes president). The machinations of politics are mostly fake; they are performed and constructed for our psychological benefit with little tangible impact (at least for those in the intended audience). But there was nothing unreal about this scandal. It personalized an issue that no normal person could possibly experience.

It was a five-sided predicament.

Unless you view the Starr Report as a nonfiction *Fifty Shades of Grey,* the first memorable book hoping to exploit the Lewinsky scandal was *American Rhapsody,* a gonzo fiction-memoir hybrid that includes one section delivered from the perspective of Bill Clinton's penis (Philip Roth's *The Human Stain* was inspired by the controversy but establishes its own narrative). Written by Joe Eszterhas, *American Rhapsody* was widely publicized but generally unsuccessful. It depicted Clinton in a manner that seemed weirdly self-congratulatory—the book opens with the author having a grunge-era phone conversation with *Rolling Stone* editor Jann Wenner about how the newly elected president was "one of us," which he translates to mean, "the real deal: undiluted, uncut rock and roll." The idea (I think) was to comically boil the imbroglio down to its allegedly essential truth, which (I suspect) was that all powerful men are driven and controlled by their sex drive, which (I suppose) is at least partially true. [I am forced to use a lot of qualifiers because *American Rhapsody* isn't very clear about its purpose.] But a much, much clearer version of how sex informs what we feel about reality can be seen in Eszterhas's screenwriting, most notably 1992's *Basic Instinct.*

Like so much from this era, *Basic Instinct* is better to remember than to rewatch. The film you imagine in your mind is closer to its original intent than the film that actually exists. The film in your mind is an erotic thriller; the film that exists is more like a comedy. This is the underrated brilliance of the Eszterhas writing style: His work begins as controversy and evolves into satire, so it succeeds twice. Twenty years after its release, the dialogue in *Basic Instinct* often resembles *Mr. Show*. The narrative details are awkward, except when they're straight-up ridiculous. But don't think about what the movie *Basic Instinct* literally is. Think about the movie you remember (or—if you've never seen it—imagine the movie I'm about to describe in a best-case scenario): A troubled San Francisco cop is investigating the ice-pick murder of a rock star. All clues point to the victim's girlfriend, a beautiful bisexual novelist (Sharon Stone) whose book perfectly mirrors the grisly actions of the murder. When questioned by authorities, she shows up for the interrogation without underwear and argues that she obviously can't be the murderer because she's *so obviously* the murderer ("I'd have to be pretty stupid to write a book about killing and then kill somebody the way I described in my book," she says before flashing her vulva at Jerry Seinfeld's downstairs neighbor). The cop (played by Michael Douglas, the only actor who could possibly be in this movie) starts having *a lot* of intense sex with the novelist while still trying to prove she is, in fact, a diabolical murderer (this paradox does not seem to particularly bother him). Virtually everyone in the story has killed someone in the distant past, so no character is above reproach; woozy Hitchcockian music reminds us that every unassuming person is potentially evil. A jealous lesbian (Stone's crazy-eyed lover) tries to kill Douglas with a motor vehicle, but she ends up killing herself instead (Stone cries when she hears about the accident, humanizing her for the first and only time). We eventually discover that the original rock-star murder was possibly committed by the cop's psychologist (whom Douglas was also sleeping with), even though this makes little logical sense and is subsequently contradicted by the film's final scene, in which we realize that Stone keeps an ice pick under her bed (thereby suggesting she either intends to kill Douglas in the near future or that she harbors some relatively untraditional methods of household tool storage).

At the time of its release, the most vocal criticism of *Basic Instinct* came from the homosexual community. The argument was that portraying lesbian characters as psychopathic killers implied that all lesbians were psychopathic killers, and that this would make people afraid of lesbians. [Remember, it was 1992. This was what people worried about.] A secondary critique was that *Basic Instinct* was misogynistic, an accusation habitually directed at movies in which unrealistic women attempt to destroy Michael Douglas's life (other films in this category include *Fatal Attraction* and *Disclosure*). A third criticism was that the film was simultaneously exploitative and reactionary: Despite an avalanche of nudity and eroticism, it subtextually connected loveless intercourse with depraved violence, latently promoting puritan ideals (this is the same academic criticism invariably chucked at teen horror flicks). A fourth criticism was that it glamorized smoking. A fifth was that Camille Paglia seemed to like it way too much. I suppose all of those attacks are quasi-valid. Still, the most interesting thing about *Basic Instinct* falls far outside its alleged problems. There is no question over who the villain in this movie is supposed to be: The villain is Sharon Stone's character, Catherine Tramell. There's no confusion on this point. "She's brilliant, she's beautiful, she's rich, she's bisexual," *Basic Instinct* director Paul Verhoeven remarked at the time. "I see her as a special edition of the devil." Granted, it's odd that Verhoeven imagines "a special edition of the devil" to be the female combination of four mostly positive qualities. But *why* he thinks the way he thinks is not the issue; what matters is that Verhoeven absolutely and irrefutably projects Tramell as the antagonist in this production. No one watches *Basic Instinct* and thinks Sharon Stone is a good person. No one argues that she's the counterintuitive hero. She does not deserve sympathy. Yet she still generates empathy. Audiences may root against her, but they don't want her to go to prison. They want her to get away with murder. They view her actions as less insane than they plainly are. And this is because Catherine Tramell's crimes are not motivated by love. Her crimes are motivated by lust.

I concede this feels backward.

I concede that our natural inclination should be to feel more tolerance for a character who kills for love. A love-driven murder seems more classically humane. But here's the thing: Love is significantly less crazy than lust. Love is a mildly irrational combination of complex feelings; lust is a totally irrational experience that ignores complexity on purpose. Tramell is never driven by love. Like some kind of amorous apex predator, she is driven by the insatiability of her lust, which we unconsciously understand as something beyond her control. She exists in a constant state of super-arousal, and that makes her mentally vulnerable (while still remaining sinister). There's a long history of this in the erotic-thriller genre. Take 1981's *Body Heat*: It somehow seems reasonable for William Hurt to throw a chair through a glass door to get his paws on Kathleen Turner, because his destruction is driven by lust. We relate to his unhinged reaction. We want it to happen. It's electrifying. However, our feelings toward both parties change as their relationship deepens (and they start plotting to murder Turner's husband). That same year, Jack Nicholson and Jessica Lange illuminated a similar dissonance in *The Postman Always Rings Twice* (their illicit, rapey intercourse is wrong yet explicable, but the ensuing relationship is explicable yet wrong). People make terrible decisions when they are in love, but they usually *know* those decisions are bad; they make those decisions anyway, only to look back later with all the predictable regret. But people consumed by lust make *no* decisions. They just react. It's neither emotional nor intellectual; it's physical and unmanageable. It is, I suppose, the most basic instinct there is.

It's hard to say if Stone's disquieting superpower in *Basic Instinct* was her own conscious intent and a product of her acting ability, particularly since she's appeared in about forty movies since *Basic Instinct* and was only good in one of them (*Casino*). It may have been a combination of timing and chance. But that doesn't make the performance any less amazing: Her character is simultaneously calculating and out of control. She can write books and make witty banter and lie to policemen, but she can't stop herself from killing everything she fucks. It's a one-dimensional compulsion that informs every aspect of her life. And that makes her seem more human than she actually is.

If you believe Christopher Andersen's low-rent 1999 book *Bill and Hillary: The Marriage,* Bill Clinton would often "gush" to friends about his favorite scene from *Basic Instinct,* which was (of course) the famous interrogation/vagina scene. Stone and Mr. Clinton have always remained tangentially connected, sometimes publicly (they've worked together on multiple charities, most notably for AIDS research) and sometimes speculatively (there were always unfounded rumors of a Clinton-Stone affair, almost to the point where even dogmatic Democrats seemed titillated by the star power of the premise). The consensus now holds that Clinton almost certainly wanted to have sex with Stone and that Sharon was probably up for it, but it just never came together. Here again: an exceedingly nineties problem. Very *Sliding Doors.* Tori Amos and Trent Reznor had the same missed connection.

It's almost too easy to look back at a former president and insist he's fascinating, because any life that culminates with that specific job is going to require a handful of unorthodox, contradictory traits (even Gerald Ford deserves more attention than he gets). But Clinton's textbook hyperthymia pushes this to another level. He's the kind of man you could trust to lead the world, but not to drive your wife to the airport. He was a tireless, talkative, highly functioning sex addict. When his affair with Lewinsky was on the verge of exploding nationally, he continued to deny its existence to every single person he worked with except for Dick Morris (his one political advisor who viewed the universe amorally). What he told Morris was this: "Ever since I got here to the White House, I've had to shut my body down—sexually, I mean. But I screwed up with this girl. I didn't do what they said I did, but I may have done so much that I can't prove my innocence." It's an explanation that embodies so much of what made Clinton the figure he will always be. He describes his libido like a world-class athlete coping with an ACL injury; he suggests that there are elements of real innocence within his undeniable guilt; he admits his deepest fears are ultimately pragmatic. [Now, granted, this is a secondhand quote from someone remembering a phone conversation that happened over a decade ago, and it might be a paraphrase—but a sentiment like "I've had to shut my body down" is so deeply bizarre that no one could misremember those words in any other way. Moreover, Dick Morris is the type of guy who would lie about a lot of things, but not something like this (where there was no personal benefit to him). In this scenario, he's probably being more honest than necessary.]

If described to someone with no memory of the recent past, the villain in the Lewinsky scandal seems stupidly obvious: We have a married, serial adulterer who receives multiple blow jobs (in the Oval Office) from a powerless subordinate half his age. He lies about it to the entire world, is exposed as a liar (and admits this on television), is impeached by the House of Representatives, and jeopardizes both the reputation of the office and the memory of every positive thing he accomplished as president. It should be a simple equation. But it isn't. Clinton's impeachment worked to his short-term political advantage. Though the impeachment charges were technically for perjury and obstruction of justice, the trial was perceived as a sanction for sexual impropriety; the public saw this as excessive and unjust. [Only about one third of Americans saw the impeachment charges as valid, which isn't that far removed from the percentage of Americans who *always* feel the president should be impeached.] The larger vilification was ultimately split five ways. Mr. Clinton, of course, was first against the wall. But Monica Lewinsky was next, and she was hammered just as aggressively (and with much less justification). So was Linda Tripp, Lewinsky's comically untelegenic gal pal who coerced her into detailing the affair while secretly taping their phone conversations. So was Kenneth Starr, the obsessive lawyer who spent most of the nineties trying to destroy the Clinton administration and forced the American public to participate in his quest. And so was Hillary Clinton, a person who did nothing wrong (but whose willingness to accept the actions of her husband eroded her status as a feminist and validated the perception that her marriage was nothing more than a loveless *House of Cards* agreement).

Had this been a more impersonal transgression—say, for treason or election fraud—it would be easier to understand who deserved the black fedora. The margins of the law would be the only thing that mattered. But this was a sexual transgression, and that complicates everything else. It taps into feelings that are impossible to separate from our own experience. Social activists are constantly trying to convince the world that personal actions can have political consequence, but this kind of gossip presented the opposite condition; this was a rare instance in which people instantaneously personalized a political drama that was detached from who they were or what they did. It caused them to think about the news in the way they traditionally thought about regular romantic life. It caused them to consider newsmakers as sexual beings. And as a result, feelings about who deserved to be hated in this circumstance were (at least partially) based on the worst possible criteria: what these people happened to look like, and how much they talked about it.

Nothing twists and obscures day-to-day human existence as much as physical attraction. It pushes our minds in every direction simultaneously; it makes people more and less popular at the same time. Being attractive is like being famous—people will listen to you longer, convince themselves that what you're saying is more interesting than it actually is, and laugh at jokes that aren't funny. It's also a justification for randomly hating someone, or for questioning the legitimacy of his or her merits and eroding whatever compassion that person might deserve (this is because beautiful people are never supposed to complain about anything). If you're single, it's important to be thin and well groomed (because this gives you a competitive romantic advantage); if you're already in a committed relationship, it's better to be a little overweight and casually disheveled (because this makes you less artificial to those who no longer view you as romantic competition). The way people look is so central to how we live (and how we respond to interpersonal conflict) that we've managed to collectively underrate its import. We all concede that appearances matter way more than they should, but we try not to dwell on this reality in practical conversation; somehow, it seems superficial to directly address how much beauty and ugliness inform consciousness. Instead we use less direct language to make the same soft points and draw the same soft conclusions. This complicates problems that are already complicated.

Case in point: This is a book about villainy. I am writing about villains (or, in some cases, perceived villains). However, I'm not writing about serial killers. This is because serial killers don't seem like villains; they seem subhuman. When examined with any degree of distance, they are depicted as either inarguably evil or criminally insane. There's a density to their personality but not to their character; if you write about Ed Gein or Albert Fish, you're mostly just cataloging the gruesomeness of their violence or the darkness of their damaged childhoods; there's almost always a sexual component, but the sex is intertwined with the depravity of their sickness. However, there's one glaring exception to this: Ted Bundy. Bundy killed and raped at least thirty women. His origin story and his psychological profile are similar to those who shared his appetites (to be fair, he was probably a little smarter than most serial killers, but only slightly—he managed to get into the University of Puget Sound law school, but his LSAT scores were average and he never finished his degree). Sometimes he would just break into coeds' apartments and bludgeon them to death while they slept. He was a brutal killing machine. Yet this is not the image of Bundy that exists in the cultural imagination. This is not what people talk about when they reference Bundy as a metaphor. Bundy is best known for being the *handsome* serial killer. [When Joyce Carol Oates wrote about Bundy in 1994, she called him "eerily glorified."] He is mostly remembered for one magnetic aspect of his criminal history: his ability to "seduce" women into following him into secluded areas so that he could murder them in private. His "seduction" technique essentially involved pretending he had a broken arm, asking random women for help with his stranded vehicle, and then hitting them in the head with a crowbar (there's four hours of audio tape in which Bundy describes this process in cold detail, a series of confessions now used by the FBI for interview training). I suppose this is not so much seduction as it is straightforward lying. However, it clearly did work; his female victims did believe his lies. Now, we will never know how much of that success was directly due to his physical appearance. But it played a role.

Bundy wasn't Taylor Kitsch (or even Mark Harmon, who portrayed Bundy in the 1986 made-for-TV movie *The Deliberate Stranger*). But he didn't look like a serial killer. I'm not sure what "looking like a serial killer" would even constitute, but I know it doesn't mean a guy who resembles Ted Bundy. And this is something that Bundy himself realized. He knew that being relatively attractive gave him illogical advantages. In 1977, Bundy was being held in Garfield County Jail in Colorado, awaiting trial on a murder charge (he'd already been convicted on a kidnapping charge). He escaped. How did he escape? He jumped out of a second-story window in the courthouse law library, where he was allowed to prepare for his upcoming trial. He was allowed to study in the nonsecure library, all by himself, without handcuffs or leggings. Granted, no one realized (at the time) how dangerous Bundy was. But it still seems odd that a convicted kidnapper charged with murder would be placed in such an easily exploitable position. It was as if the local authorities looked at Ted and simply thought, This is not the kind of person who escapes from jail. Charisma goes a long way.

Seemingly every serial murderer is also a sex offender. The relationship is almost one-to-one; the fact that Bundy focused on college girls and dabbled in necrophilia is not unique. What is different, however, is the way Bundy's deviancy is normalized by the rest of society. This is a person who once tried to rip off a woman's nipple with his teeth. He assaulted another woman with a medical speculum. His depravity was beyond the pale. Yet how was this behavior described by psychologists? According to Bundy biographer Ann Rule, the psychiatric conclusion was that Bundy had a "fear of being humiliated in his relationships with women." This almost makes him seem like a normal, insecure dude. In the final hours before his 1989 execution, Bundy claimed his pathology was created by an addiction to pornography. This is almost certainly untrue; Bundy happened to be talking to an anti-porn advocate when he made this specific declaration, and he'd blamed many other entities in the past (including the victims themselves). But it was a savvy lie. It further galvanized the relationship between Bundy and mainstream sexuality. It made him seem less like a fiend and more like a deeply troubled person (which—in this case—is far more desirable). Sometimes people writing about Bundy will mention how it was ironic that, as a college student in Washington, he wrote a manual to help women protect themselves from rapists. This is, I suppose, one example of irony. But I don't think people would use the word *irony* if a young Jeffrey Dahmer had written a handbook on how to avoid sexually confused cannibals. Dahmer wasn't handsome enough. We'd use the words "predictably diabolical" instead.

If this seems like an extreme, convoluted way of arguing that "attractive people are treated differently from normal people," I apologize. I'm a weird-looking person, so perhaps I have an unconscious bias against the beautiful. But I don't think that's what's happening here. In fact, I suspect my true bias mirrors the bias of almost everyone I've ever met: I view reality through the lens of someone predisposed toward treating attractive people differently than everyone else (and mostly to their benefit). If Kate Upton pulled a gun on me, I don't think I'd beg for mercy. I think I'd try to make conversation. "You're threatening to shoot me," I'd remark. "That's so empowering."

"It's not the sex. It's the lying."

I wonder how many times I heard this in 1998. It was the one-sentence way to express the conventional wisdom about the Clinton-Lewinsky scandal, and it seemed so *reasonable*. (Had Facebook existed in '98, it would have been the default status update for every boring person you know.) In just seven words, the sentiment made a clear argument: The fact that Clinton had an affair was not appropriate, but the fact that he lied about this affair was momentous and unacceptable. It was an intolerable decision. So this is what people said: "It's not the sex. It's the lying." Which was totally idiotic and completely untrue.

Presidents lie all the time. Really *great* presidents lie. Abraham Lincoln managed to end slavery in America partially by deception. (In an 1858 debate, he flatly insisted that he had no intention of abolishing slavery in states where it was already legal—he had to say this in order to slow the tide of secession.) Franklin Roosevelt lied about the U.S. position of neutrality until we entered World War II after the attack on Pearl Harbor. (Though the public and Congress believed his public pledge of impartiality, he was already working in secret with Winston Churchill and selling arms to France.) Ronald Reagan lied about Iran-Contra so much that it now seems like he was honestly confused. Politically, the practice of lying is essential. By the time the Lewinsky story broke, Clinton had already lied about many, many things. (He'd openly lied about his level of commitment to gay rights during the '92 campaign.) The presidency is not a job for an honest man. It's way too complex. If honesty drove the electoral process, Jimmy Carter would have served two terms and the 2008 presidential race would have been a dead heat between Ron Paul and Dennis Kucinich. Expressing outrage over a president's lack of honesty is like getting upset over a sniper's lack of empathy: It's an integral component of the vocation. So when people said, "It's not the sex. It's the lying," they were pretending—either to themselves or for the benefit of other people. They were trying to work through this as a problem that could exist in their own life, and they were trying to reconcile how they would manage the crisis. But this was not about lying. The president of the United States of America is obviously going to lie about cheating on his wife.

It was about the sex.

For the sake of clarity, here is a super-simplified overview of what technically transpired: It's the 1990s. It's a best-case scenario for an American president. After five decades of adversarial stasis, the United States is the lone international superpower, engaged in no meaningful wars (either hot or cold). The economy is booming and the nation is safe, so people are making up problems to be worried about: the looming Y2K disaster, northern spotted owls, the absurdity of Metallica headlining Lollapalooza. Clinton is neither popular nor unpopular; his first-term Gallup approval rating is 50 percent. In 1995, Lewinsky—an affluent twenty-two-year-old child of divorce with a degree in psychology—gets an unpaid internship in the White House. The president begins flirting with her, or she begins flirting with him (probably both). On November 15 of 1995 (eleven days before becoming a full-time employee), Lewinsky encounters the president in the office of the chief of staff and somehow ends up showing him the strap of her thong underwear. Clinton has never discussed this incident, but one assumes he must have thought, This seems promising. That same night, Clinton asks Lewinsky if he can kiss her. She agrees. The affair begins in earnest. They never have traditional intercourse, but Clinton spends a lot of time investigating the texture of her bosom and receives a boatload of fellatio, some of which occurs while he is on the telephone with a member of Congress. As one might imagine, this is an unconventional relationship. At first, Clinton does not let Lewinsky bring him to orgasm, claiming he needs to trust her more. Eventually his trust grows (and this will be his downfall). On March 31, Clinton inserts a cigar into Lewinsky's vagina, returns the cigar to his mouth, and supposedly says, "It tastes good." They exchange inexpensive, inappropriate gifts that reflect the gap in their maturity (he gives her things like Walt Whitman's *Leaves of Grass* while she gives him a souvenir coffee mug featuring the words SANTA MONICA). Clinton tells Lewinsky they must keep their relationship ultraprivate; she promises to tell no one, but she is twenty-two years old, so "no one" means her therapist and her mom and a bunch of her friends over e-mail. Sensing (realizing?) the stupidity of his situation and realizing (fearing?) how it could affect his reelection, Clinton distances himself from Lewinsky. She is transferred to a job at the Pentagon on April 16. On May 24, Clinton explains that they can no longer have a sexual relationship; she tries to emotionally persuade him otherwise, but he rejects her pleas.

Once the affair is over, things become more fragile and about a thousand times more political. A distraught Lewinsky begins confiding in one of her Pentagon coworkers, Linda Tripp. Tripp is roughly twice Lewinsky's age and had previously worked for G. H. W. Bush. On the advice of a friend in the publishing industry, Tripp begins surreptitiously taping phone conversations with Lewinsky, probing her for details about the affair. This is where things get confusing. Tripp ends up delivering these tapes to Kenneth Starr, who wants them for a byzantine purpose: If Starr can prove that Clinton had an affair with Lewinsky, it will mean Clinton had lied under oath in a deposition involving Paula Jones, an Arkansas woman suing Clinton for sexual harassment that had allegedly occurred while he was still a governor in 1991. Now, what makes all this so twisted is that Starr's original motive for investigating Clinton had nothing to do with anything sexual. Starr was looking into the Clinton family's financial involvement in a corrupt 1970s land deal (the mostly forgotten "Whitewater controversy") and the quasi-mysterious suicide of Vince Foster (who'd briefly worked as a White House counsel before shooting himself in 1993). So what we have, in essence, is a lawyer (Starr) failing to prove impropriety on one issue (Whitewater) and subsequently attempting to continue the pursuit of his target (Clinton) through totally different means (Lewinsky), based on an unrelated impropriety (Jones) that happened sometime in between. The linchpin is Tripp, who has both the incriminating audio cassettes and knowledge of a blue dress in Lewinsky's closet that includes remnants of Clinton's semen (like I said—he trusted her eventually). Tripp convinces Lewinsky not to dry-clean the dress, as this DNA could be exchanged for immunity (which Lewinsky needs, because she'd lied under oath in the Jones case, too).

The story is broken by the Drudge Report, substantiated by the *Washington Post,* and then reported everywhere. Clinton is asked about the allegation and lies so directly ("I did not have sexual relations with that woman") that it seems as if he must feel secure in his safety; even casual detractors who are certain of his guilt concede there must be no proof (because no tangibly guilty man would lie so brazenly). But the blue dress cannot be denied. Lewinsky turns the garment over to the prosecution in July; a month later, Clinton goes on TV and admits to the affair. It is the lowest point of his presidency. In December, he is impeached by the House of Representatives. It appears as though his sexual appetite has destroyed his career, just as his oldest enemies always predicted. Yet the impeachment has the opposite effect. It not only fails, but also dramatically improves Clinton's perception and likability. During the week before Christmas, his approval rating hits 73 percent, the highest it will ever be.

That December, Clinton's unprecedented approval did not feel nearly as strange as it does in retrospect. At the time, the explanation for why he became so popular was framed as a compliment to the American people: It (supposedly) proved that the populace was more sophisticated than the media and the government. Lewinsky coverage was ubiquitous, and the potential consequences of impeachment were massive, but—given their sudden support for the man at the scandal's center—it seemed as though normal citizens realized that this fiasco was not critical to the fabric of American politics. It was just gossip that turned out to be true. But that's precisely why it matters.

"Nobody roots for Goliath." This is what Wilt Chamberlain used to say about himself (and he must have said it constantly, because I don't think I've ever read a single overview of his career that didn't repeat that quote verbatim). The reasons Chamberlain was vilified could be a book unto itself; he remains the gold standard for an athlete who was both unstoppable and unpopular. Normally, one would have expected the animosity toward Wilt to fade over time, and certainly in the wake of his 1999 death. We should all love him now, because dead men are loved. The things that exasperated Chamberlain's critics—his obsession with numbers, his unabashed selfishness, the inability to elevate his game when it mattered most—should be secondary footnotes to his overall body of work (a statistical monolith that certifies him as the most dominant basketball player of his or any generation). But Wilt made one final mistake, eighteen years after his retirement: In 1991, he published a book titled *A View from Above,* in which he claimed to have had sex with twenty thousand women. By his own mathematical calculation, this would be an average of 1.2 women a day from the time he was fifteen until he was fifty.

Now, this feat is obviously impossible. It was just an example of Wilt trying to be provocative. But people really hated this. They still remember it, even though the book itself is forgotten and out of print. And what's crazy is that Wilt's life *did* involve an insane amount of sex (not 1.2 women a day for thirty-five years, but more than any reasonable humanoid possibly requires). It was one of the central qualities of his personality; he was a lifelong bachelor and a serial womanizer. If the real number of his sexual conquests could somehow be tabulated, it would still astonish anyone who isn't a porn star. The number "20,000" is not what people find distasteful. What people find distasteful is that the source of that number was Chamberlain. If Bill Russell had given an interview and said, "You know, I won more NBA championships than Wilt, but that guy slept with twenty thousand women," Chamberlain's approval rating would have soared (while Russell would be viewed as both magnanimous and jealous). We'd think of Wilt the way we think of Bob Marley, an introvert who sired eleven children with seven women (but is still adored). If Jerry West had claimed in his autobiography that "I was really embarrassed by Wilt as a teammate. This is a guy who slept with twenty thousand women," people would view Chamberlain as compelling and complex (while West would seem self-righteous and lame). The number "twenty thousand" wouldn't be any less implausible, but the impact would be totally different. It would change the way we think about Chamberlain as a basketball player, even though his sex life and his rebounding have no link whatsoever.

So this is something to remember: The talking matters almost as much as the fucking (and sometimes more).

In 2012, Greil Marcus was interviewed at length by Simon Reynolds, originally for an article in the *Guardian* but ultimately for the *Los Angeles Review of Books*. Marcus and Reynolds remain significant pop critics, but neither regularly writes about the straightfor-ward sound of music anymore (or at least not in a conventional, blurb-o-centric context). They mostly write about cultural pol-itics, and sometimes just politics. Marcus is the most academi-cally respected rock writer of the twentieth century. His opinions are concurrently predictable and inventive: His values are exactly what you'd expect from someone who studied political science at Berkley during the 1960s, but they're delivered through a dense, wide-lens model that's totally unique to him. The postmodern political figure Marcus hates most is Ronald Reagan. The post-modern political figure he seems to appreciate the most—despite some internal confliction—is Bill Clinton. Here's something he said to Reynolds in that interview:

> For all of [Clinton's] failings, the way he put all that he'd done that was good in jeopardy and allowed his enemies to derail his presidency by fucking around with Monica Lewinsky . . . the way he just blew it, saying "Fuck it—I want this," which is very human. For all of his awful compromises and the terrible deci-sions he made, I really *like* Bill Clinton. I supported him whole-heartedly from beginning to end. And he made me proud to be part of this country.

On the surface, this is pretty straightforward: An intellectual born in 1945 supports a liberal president despite that president's personal failings. You can see the struggle inside Marcus's brain, but you also see his rationalization and his larger point. It's a suc-cinct summation of how most pro-Clinton partisans have emo-tively decided to remember his two terms in office. But it's still weird. It's weird that within this five-sided dilemma—within the human pentagon of Bill, Hillary, Lewinsky, Tripp, and Starr—the person who is perceived the least negatively is the person who was the most irrefutably immoral.

Let's consider the other four players involved. What, exactly, did Monica Lewinsky do wrong? Well, she knowingly had oral sex with a married man, and she lied about it. But she was unmarried, very young, and operating from a powerless position. Yet people still hated her and joked about the size of her ass. What did Hillary do wrong? Absolutely nothing—but the takeaway was still damaging to her iconography. [There's a scene from the third season of *The Sopranos* in which Edie Falco and three of her friends discuss Hillary in 2001, ultimately concluding that, "She's a role model for all of us." This seems like a compliment until you realize that "us" constitutes four unhappy women who are trapped in relationships with philandering criminals.] What did Kenneth Starr do wrong? He did his job so aggressively that it seemed unfair and driven by bias, which it was. His obituary will describe him as a weasel. Linda Tripp? She pretended to be Monica's friend, taped private phone conversations, deceived those who trusted her, held grudges, and literally looked like a witch (which, I must add, was not her fault). Tripp is the most classically vilified of the five involved parties—she was both the catalyst and the least personally involved. [Here again, we see the bottom line: A villain is the person who knows the most and cares the least.] Even on the far right she has few defenders. Betraying a friend is hard to forgive, but feigning friendship *for the sole purpose of betrayal* is basically unforgivable.

This leaves us with Bill Clinton, a man who did many things wrong. He cheated on his wife. He cheated on his wife with a subordinate and used his power as collateral. He cheated on his wife (with a subordinate) and lied about it to almost everyone on the planet. He cheated on his wife (with a subordinate), lied to everyone, and did so while serving as leader of the world's only superpower. He cheated on his wife (with a subordinate), lied about it, diminished the presidency, and actively convinced a much younger person to fall in love with him while having no intention of ever reciprocating the feeling. Even within the illicit relationship, he was sexually selfish. The magnitude of his recklessness is almost unfathomable—the biggest political scandal of the nineties could have been completely avoided if he'd just disappeared into his bedroom for ten minutes and masturbated. It's hard to imagine a more self-destructive decision from a person whose decisions matter so much. And yet . . . Bill Clinton is not the villain here. I mean, he *is* the villain, but no one feels that way unless forced to somehow describe why (or how) he should be viewed in any other context. His defining failure did not define him. There are a handful on the extreme Left who despise Bill Clinton, but that's because he made economic compromises; there are many on the Right who will hate him forever, but they felt that way in 1993. Bill Clinton got away with cheating on his wife for fleeting, one-sided gratification. There is no disputing this. By the time he spoke at the 2012 DNC convention his Gallup approval rating was 63 percent *with women.*

Now, to a certain kind of reader, the explanation as to why we ultimately don't care that Bill Clinton put the country at risk in exchange for a dozen loveless blow jobs is obvious and easy: "It is because he is a man, and there's an engrained double standard that allows men to behave in this manner." It's hard to discount that argument, although I guess I (kind of) do. It was a factor, but certainly not the central factor. It mattered that he was a man, but it mattered more that he was a *handsome* man. And it mattered even more that he was a handsome man who never, ever spoke about what actually happened.

America is a looks-based, superficial society. Everyone accepts this, and only the naïve disagree. Yet we still (somehow) underrate its cultural persuasion. Physical appearance is the most important element of almost every human interaction we have (not the *only* element, but the one that is most fundamental and expansive). One of my deepest fears about democracy is that—for the rest of my life—presidential elections will be dominated by whichever candidate is more conventionally attractive (in the last six presidential elections, the younger candidate has won five times, a stark contrast to the historical record). This is the knowable consequence of a mediated universe. We have a black president, and we could easily have a female president; I think we could have a black female president, if Oprah Winfrey got into politics. But could there ever be a *dwarf* president? No way. Tyrion Lannister couldn't carry New Hampshire. Could a modern-day Thomas Jefferson win a primary if he also had a severe skull deformity? Nay. Such a scenario will not happen in my lifetime, or in the lifetime of this book. And remember—the presidency is (normally) a totally nonsexual job. It's a situation in which there's no biological imperative to gravitate toward the more attractive candidate. It's not difficult to project the unconscious impact the president's charisma and appearance had in a scenario that actually *was* about sex. It mattered way more than logic, and it was amplified by something else that mattered almost as much: Clinton, a man who never seemed able to stop talking about anything, remained forever silent about the only thing everyone wanted to know.

Bill Clinton's autobiography, *My Life,* is 1,056 pages long. Within those 1,056 pages, the word *Lewinsky* is mentioned seventeen times (nineteen if you include the index). By comparison, the word *football* is somehow used thirty-five times. He fleetingly references Lewinsky like a policy problem that's too complicated for any layperson to comprehend; if an alien attempted to understand who Lewinsky was from everything Bill Clinton said or wrote about her, the extent of the alien's data would be that Monica was, in fact, a woman. It has become clear that this situation is something he is simply never going to explain. We will never know his personal view of the events. Most of the other parties have caved. Monica talked on HBO (in the documentary *Monica in Black and White,* she allowed an audience of strangers to ask how she felt about being "America's blow job queen"). Tripp talked to Ken Starr, and Ken Starr talked to everybody. Hillary would talk if she had anything to say. But Bill Clinton talked to no one, and that saved him. Either by accident or to his credit, he understood the awkward paradox of human sexuality: Everyone's obsessed with it, but no one wants to hear about it. All it does is make them hate you.

As I type this essay, I find myself dwelling on two specific memories, both of which seem as if they should be reconstituted into some kind of symbolic conclusion. But whenever I try to make this happen, I realize they are only connected because of me.

Still, I have no way around this. There is no way around myself unless I become somebody else.

The first memory is a phone call from 1998. I was working at a newspaper, avoiding whatever it was I was being paid to do. I was killing time on the telephone with an outspoken Democrat I barely knew; she was expressing histrionic disappointment with Bill Clinton, because the news of his affair had just broken. Neither of us was trying to prove anything. I was not interviewing her. We were just talking. But she casually said something I will never forget: "I could almost understand this if he'd done it with Sharon Stone," she told me, "but not with this fat pig." I was not offended by this opinion, even though I know I should have been. I intuitively understood what she meant. I thought it was a terrible argument (especially coming from a self-described feminist), but I could tell it was her honest reaction. And there was something about the way she said those words—and the way they didn't affect me—that made me wonder if perhaps this is how people think about almost everything (and that maybe I thought this way, too, against my will). Whenever someone says something that's both realistic and abhorrent, it makes me suspect everyone else is lying about everything else.

The second memory starts the way most of my Clinton-era memories start: I was in love with a woman who was not in love with me, even though we spent all our time together. Almost arbitrarily, she became attracted to one of my lifelong friends;

she appreciated his brain and loved his car. She asked him to take her to *Basic Instinct,* which had just opened in theaters (a scant ten days after Clinton had wrapped up his party's nomination on Super Tuesday). Now, this particular friend really goes for the jugular. He is a high achiever and a natural-born objectivist—he believed everything in *Atlas Shrugged* long before he knew such a book could even exist. That might explain what happened next. Two days after seeing the movie, he asked me a difficult, practical question: "Since you are not having sex with this woman and she has no intentions of having sex with you, is it okay if *I* have sex with her, since that is what she obviously wants?" [I'm paraphrasing his words here, but just barely.] I suppose I could have said no (or at least said "yes" in a way that would have *seemed* like "no"). But that's not what I did. I assured my friend it was totally okay, and I unsuccessfully pretended not to care while successfully drinking eighteen Busch beers. It was the closest I'll ever be to understanding Hillary Clinton. What I thought at the time is the same as what I think now: "Well, go ahead. You might as well have sex with her. You've already seen *Basic Instinct* together. You're halfway there."

It's never about the lying. It's about those rare things that are actually true, just like everything else.

ELECTRIC FUNERAL

If you're reading this book in order, you've just finished a section about Bill Clinton, the forty-second president of the United States. Unless this book has survived far longer than I anticipate, most readers will picture Clinton as a living, breathing mammal. You remember where you were when he was elected in 1992 and the condition of your life during his two-term tenure. His time as POTUS might feel more recent than it actually is (and perhaps that makes you feel strange). But there's another chunk of readers who had a different experience when they read that essay (and the size of that chunk will get progressively larger for the rest of eternity). Those in the second camp recall Clinton only vaguely, or not at all. You know he was once the president in the same way you know Woodrow Wilson was once the president. It feels like something that happened long ago. That makes you different from those in the first camp (and for a lot of different reasons). And there's one specific divergence that matters more than most people think: If you're in that first group, your parents worried about how you were affected by the media—and what they worried about was the *content* you were consuming. If you were born in 1960, your parents worried about Black Sabbath; if you were born in 1970, they worried about *Porky's*; if you were born in 1980, they worried about *Beavis and Butt-head*. Their fear was that you'd be changed by the images you saw and the messages you heard, and perhaps they believed that content needed to be regulated. Their concern was tethered to the message. But if you were born after 1990, this is not the case. Instead, your parents were (or are) primarily worried about the *medium* through which all of those things are accessed. The medium is far more problematic than the message. When a father looks at his typically unfocused four-year-old hypnotically immersed with an iPad for three straight hours, he thinks, "Somehow, I know this is bad." Is does not matter that the four-year-old might be learning essential skills on that device; what matters is the way such an intense, insular, digital experience will irreparably alter the way he'll experience the non-simulated world. It's normalizing something that was once abnormal, and it's distancing the child from reality. It will transmogrify his brainstem into the opening credit sequence of Gaspar Noé's *Enter the Void*. And the worst part is that there is no other option. If a father stops his son from embracing the online universe, he's stopping him from becoming a competitive adult; it's like refusing to teach him how to drive a car or boil water. You may worry about all the ancillary consequences, but you can't take away the experience. Avoiding the Internet is akin to avoiding everything that matters. This is even true for adults. An author I know once explained why writing became so much more difficult in the twenty-first century: "The biggest problem in my life," he said, "is that my work machine is also my pornography delivery machine."

The future makes the rules.

The future makes the rules, so there's no point in being mad when the future wins. In fact, the easiest way for any cutthroat person to succeed is to instinctively (and relentlessly) side with the technology of tomorrow, even if that technology is distasteful. Time will eventually validate that position. The only downside is that—until that validation occurs—less competitive people will find you annoying and unlikable.

The future will retire undefeated, but it always makes a terrible argument for its own success. The argument is inevitably some version of this: "You might not like where we're going, and tomorrow might be worse than yesterday. But it's still going to happen, whether you like it or not. It's inevitable." And this is what people hate. They hate being *dragged* into the future, and they hate the technocrats who remind them that this is always, always, always happening. We tend to dislike cultural architects who seem *excited* that the world is changing, particularly when those architects don't seem particularly concerned whether those changes make things worse. They know they will end up on the right side of history, because the future always wins. These are people who have the clearest understanding of what technology can do, but no emotional stake in how its application will change the lives of people who aren't exactly like them. [They know the most and care the least . . . and they kind of think that's funny.] Certainly, this brand of technophobia has always existed. As early as 1899, people like H. G. Wells were expressing apprehension about a future "ruled by an aristocracy of organizers, men who manage railroads and similar vast enterprises." But this is different. This is about the kind of person who will decide what that future is.

*   *   *

Early in the third season of *The Sopranos,* there's a two-episode subplot in which my favorite character (Christopher Moltisanti) sticks up a charity concert at Rutgers University (the musical headliner is Jewel). What's most interesting about this robbery is the person who hands over the money: The role of the ter- rified box office clerk is portrayed by an unknown actor named Mario Lavandeira. He has only two lines, but the scene—when viewed retroactively—is more culturally significant than every- thing else that happens in that particular episode. This is because Mario Lavandeira would soon rename himself Perez Hilton and become the first authentically famous blogger, which (of course) made him the most hated blogger of his generation.

[There are no famous bloggers who aren't hated.]

Perez Hilton once claimed that 8.82 million people read his website within a twenty-four-hour period in 2007. The magnitude of this number was disputed by competing gossip sources, but those critics came off like the type of person who wants to argue over the specific number of people killed during the Holocaust: They missed the point entirely. Even if Hilton was tripling his true traffic figures, the audience for what he was doing was massive. And what he was doing was terrible. It was objectively immoral. The crux of his publishing empire was based around defacing copyrighted photos of celebrities (often to imply they were addicted to cocaine). Other central pursuits included the outing of gay celebrities (Perez himself is homosexual) and publishing unauthorized photos of teen celebrities who may or may not be wearing underwear. The apex of his career was when he broke the news of Fidel Castro's death, a report mildly contradicted by Castro's unwillingness to stop living. Hilton was also a judge for the Miss USA Pageant, a referee for a WWE wrestling match, and the star of a VH1 reality show I never actually saw. [I realize Mr. Hilton would likely disagree with my overview of his career and insist that I failed to mention how he's also been involved with numerous sex-positive, pro-youth, anti-bullying initiatives. But I suspect he will totally agree with much of what I'm going to write next, mostly because it makes him look far less culpable than he probably is.]

Whenever you have an audience as large as Hilton's, there's obviously going to be a substantial swath of consumers who adore the person who built it. It would be wrong to say, "Everyone hates Perez Hilton," because that's just not true. But it's pretty hard to find an intelligent person who loves him. (Such individuals exist, but not in great numbers.) It's hard to find a thoughtful person who appreciates the way Hilton's appeal is so hyper-directed at the lowest common denominator. Even his decision to name himself after noted celebutard Paris Hilton perpetuates a desire to produce self-consciously vapid work. So this, it would seem, is why smart people hate him: Because of his blog's content. They find his ideas despicable (or so they would argue). Now, Perez would counter that accusation by charging his critics with jealousy. He (and his defenders) would claim that what people truly hate about Perez Hilton is not what he writes; it's the size of his audience and the scale of his reach. That argument is not invalid. For those who live on the Internet, the attention economy matters way more than making money or earning peer respect; there is a slice of the Web that would do *anything* to harvest Hilton's readership, even if it meant publishing photos of aborted celebrity fetuses while going bankrupt in the process. In other words, some people hate Perez for his ideas and some people hate Perez because they so desperately want to be like him. And as it turns out, both sides have a point. The reason Perez Hilton became a villain was the intersection of those two qualities: It wasn't just the content, and it wasn't just the success. It was the creeping fear that this type of content would become the *only* way any future person could be successful.

Necessity used to be the mother of invention, but then we ran out of things that were necessary. The postmodern mother of invention is desire; we don't really "need" anything new, so we only create what we *want*. This changes the nature of technological competition. Because the Internet is obsessed with its own version of non-monetary capitalism, it rewards the volume of response much more than the merits of whatever people are originally responding to. Moreover, there's no downside to creating something that repulses all those who exist outside your audience (in fact, a reasonable degree of outsider hatred usually helps). Intuitively understanding these rules, Hilton only went after the kind of pre-adult who simultaneously loved and loathed celebrity culture to an unhealthy degree; he knew that specific demographic was both expanding and underserved. It was a brilliant business model. It was like he opened a buffet restaurant that served wet garbage in a community where the population of garbage gluttons was much higher (and far more loyal) than anyone had ever realized. And this made all the normal food eaters hate him. Do they hate his product? Sure (although there are many things on the Internet far worse). Do they hate his success? Sure (although he's never been perceived as credible or particularly insightful, so the definition of his success is limited to pure populism). Do they simply think Hilton is a jerk? Yes (and perhaps he is—I have no idea). But none of those individual issues addresses the greater fear. The real reason Perez Hilton is vilified is the combination of a) what he does editorially, b) its level of public import, and c) the undeniable sense that all of this was somehow *inevitable*. Perez Hilton is a villain because he personifies the way desire-based technology drives mass culture toward primitive impulses. Any singular opinion of his work does not matter; the only thing that matters is the collective opinion, which can be dominated by a vocal, splintered minority who knows only that they want what they want. Everyone seems to understand this. And once everyone understands that this is how New Media works, it becomes normative. It becomes the main way we get information about everything (gossip or otherwise). There is no alternative option. By manipulating an audience that is complicit in the manipulation, Perez Hilton can force the rest of us to accept his version of the future.

Hilton is a technocrat, and technocrats inevitably share two unifying beliefs. The first is that they're already winning; the second is that they're going to push things forward, regardless of what that progress entails. Resistance to either principle is futile. Every day we grow closer to a full-on technocratic police state. "I don't care if you like me," Hilton has written. "I just care if you read my website." This is not exactly an original perspective; many writers feel like that, especially when they're young (Hilton was roughly twenty-four when he first experienced success). But the sentiment is disturbing when expressed by Perez. It seems like his entire objective. It's like he vividly sees the relationship between those two adversarial ideas, and everything else is built upon that foundation. And this would be totally fine, assuming we felt as if it was our decision to agree or disagree. But we don't. At this point, we can't walk away from harmful technology. We've ceded control to the machines. The upside is that the machines still have masters. The downside is that we don't usually like who those masters are.

★ ★ ★

When Kim Dotcom was arrested during a 2012 police raid of his home, I had the same series of reactions as everyone else: There's a person literally named "Kim Dotcom"? And this person is a 350-pound, egocentric German multimillionaire who never went to college? And he got famous for being a computer hacker who refers to himself as Dr. Evil? And he lives in a mansion in New Zealand? And he participates in European road races and is the world's best *Modern Warfare 3* player? And he has a beautiful wife of unknown racial origin? And his twenty-four-acre, $30 million estate is populated with life-size statues of giraffes? And he likes to be photographed in his bathtub? Everything about his biography seemed like someone trying to make fun of a Roger Moore–era James Bond movie that was too dumb to exist. I could not believe that *this* was the person the FBI decided to go after in their ongoing dream of controlling the digital future. It seemed as if they were arbitrarily penalizing a cherubic foreigner for being wealthy and ostentatious, and New Zealand eventually deemed the raid illegal.

However, the arrest turned out to be far less arbitrary than I'd thought. Dotcom owned and operated the online service Megaupload. In an interview with Kiwi investigative reporter John Campbell, Dotcom (born Kim Schmitz in 1974) described Megaupload like this: "I basically created a server where I could upload a file and get a unique link, and then I would just e-mail that link to my friend so he would then get the file. And that's how Megaupload was started. It was just a solution to a problem that still exists today." In essence, Dotcom's argument was that he simply made it easier for people to exchange and store digital files that were too large for Gmail or AOL—and when described in this simplified manner, it seems like his motives were utilitarian. But this claim is such a profound distortion of reality that it almost qualifies as a lie, even though (I suppose) it's technically true. Megaupload was a place to steal music. There was no mystery about this; if you knew what Megaupload was, you knew it was a pirating service. There appeared to be dozens of other sites exactly like it. But what I did not realize was the scope of Dotcom's empire: The week after he was arrested, downloading illegal music became almost impossible (not *totally* impossible, but at least ten times more difficult than it had been in 2011). His arrest instantly changed the entire culture of recreational music theft. For most normal adults, ripping music from the Internet went from "a little too easy" to "a little too hard." Megaupload was more central to the process of stealing copyrighted material than every other file-sharing source combined. He really *was* the man. Kim Dotcom was not some goofy eccentric being persecuted for the sins of other people. He pretty much ran the Internet (or at least the part of the Internet that people with money actually care about). He denies this, as any wise man would. But even his denials suggest a secret dominance. Here's one exchange from his conversation with Campbell, the first TV interview he gave following his arrest . . .

CAMPBELL: The FBI indictment against you alleges, and I quote, "Copyright infringement on a massive scale, with estimated harm to copyright holders well in excess of five hundred million U.S. dollars."

DOTCOM: Well, that's complete nonsense. If you read the indictment and if you hear what the Prosecution has said in court, those $500 million of damage were just music files from a two-week time period. So they are actually talking about $13 billion U.S. damages within a year, just for music downloads. The entire U.S. music industry is less than $20 billion. So how can one

> website be responsible for this amount of damage? It's
> completely mind-boggling and unrealistic.

It *is* mind-boggling. But it isn't unrealistic. While I don't doubt the FBI is using an unusually high estimate, it doesn't seem implausible that $13 billion worth of music was flowing through Megaupload's channels (assuming we pretend a CD is still worth its fourteen-dollar retail price). Ripping music is not like buying music. It's not a meditative process. When you purchase music, you make a specific choice that (in your mind) justifies the exchange of currency. When you download music illegally, there's nothing to exchange; if you can simply *think* of a record's title and you can type it semi-correctly into a search engine, there's no reason not to drop it into your iTunes. That's pretty much the entire investment—the ability to type a band name into a search field. Megaupload made stealing simple (it was far better than the previous theft iteration, the Napster-like Limewire). The downloading process took (maybe) forty-five seconds per album, and—if you elected to never listen to those songs, even once—you lost nothing. People would download albums just because they were bored. Since the advent (and fall) of Napster in 1999, consumers' relationship to music as a commodity completely collapsed. Supply became unlimited, so demand became irrelevant. A better argument from Dotcom would have been that the $13 billion he was accused of "reappropriating" was not actually $13 billion, but merely the projected value of what such exchanges would have been worth in 1998 (and only if the world had become some kind of strange musical utopia where consumers immediately purchased every single album they were remotely intrigued by).

Weirder still is that the charge of music theft isn't even the main reason media conglomerates wanted Dotcom's arrest. Their real concern was the increasing potential for the pirating of feature-length films, which is only feasible through this kind of server (relative to the size of mp3 music clips, film files are massive). The movie industry makes the music industry look like a food co-op (in 2011, global film revenue was $87 billion). Kim Dotcom clearly understood this, which prompted him to make the kind of move usually reserved for the Joker: Despite being under arrest, he wrote an open letter to the *Hollywood Reporter*, mocking the film industry's inability to understand the future of its own vehicle. His twelve-paragraph letter opens like a Tweet: "Dear Hollywood: The Internet frightens you." And he just keeps going . . .

> (*paragraph* 2): "You get so comfortable with your ways of doing business that any change is perceived as a threat. The problem is, we as a society don't have a choice: The law of human nature is to communicate more efficiently."

> (*paragraph* 4): "My whole life is like a movie. I wouldn't be who I am if it wasn't for the mind-altering glimpse at the future in *Star Wars*. I am at the forefront of creating the cool stuff that will allow creative works to thrive in an Internet age. I have the solutions to your problems. I am not your enemy."

> (*paragraph* 7): "The people of the Internet will unite. They will help me. And they are stronger than you. We will prevail in the war for Internet freedom and innovation that you have launched. We have logic, human nature and the invisible hand on our side."

The document concludes with Dotcom's signature snark: "This open letter is free of copyright. Use it freely." Technically, he's trying to forward his opinion on how copyright law should be applied, based on the principle that the laws governing ownership over intellectual property are outdated and not designed for the machinations of the Internet age. But that's not what interests me. What interests me is his personality and his leverage—and in the case of Dotcom, those qualities are connected.

If you've ever worked in an office filled with computers (which, at this point, is the only kind of office that exists), you've undoubtedly had some kind of complicated, one-sided relationship with whoever worked in the IT department. "IT" stands for "information technology." [An easy illustration of the one-sidedness of this relationship can be quickly illustrated by asking random people what the "I" and "T" literally represent in that acronym. You may be surprised by the results.] Now, there are exceptions to every rule, and I don't want to unfairly stereotype anyone. But people fucking hate IT guys. They want to knife them in the throat and pour acid in their ears. They want to see them arrested for the possession of kiddie porn.

There are two reasons why this is.

The first is that workers typically encounter IT people only when something is already wrong with their desktop (there just aren't any situations where you *want* someone to be doing things to your computer that you can't do yourself). But the second reason is the one that matters more. Regardless of their station within the office hierarchy, there's never any debate over how much power the IT department has: It's borderline infinite. They control all, and they have access to everything. They can't fire you, but they could get you fired in twenty-four hours. You may have a despotic boss who insists he won't take no for an answer, but he'll take it from an IT guy. He'll eat shit from an IT guy, day after day after day.

Specialists in information technology are the new lawyers. Long ago, lawyers realized that they could make themselves culturally essential if they made the vernacular of contracts too complex for anyone to understand except themselves. They made the language of contracts unreadable on purpose. [Easy example: I can write a book, and my editor can edit a book . . . but neither one of us can read and understand the contract that allows those things to happen.] IT workers became similarly unstoppable the moment they realized virtually every machine powering the modern world is too complicated for the average person to fix or calibrate. And they know this. This is what makes an IT guy different from you. He might make less money, he might have less social prestige, and people might look at him in the cafeteria like he's a morlock—*but he can act however he wants.* He can be nice, but only if he feels like it. He can ignore the company dress code. He can lie for no reason whatsoever (because how would anyone understand what he's lying about?). He can smoke weed at lunch, because he'll still understand your iMac better than you. It doesn't matter how he behaves: The IT department dominates technology, and technology dominates the rest of us. And this state of being creates a new kind of personality. It creates someone like Kim Dotcom, a man who's essentially an IT guy for the entire planet.

"I'm an easy target," Mr. Dotcom claims in his defense. "My flamboyance, my history as a hacker. I'm not American. I'm living somewhere in New Zealand, around the world. I have funny number plates on my cars. I'm an easy target." (Kim Dotcom drives around in luxury vehicles with license plates that read GUILTY.) There is, certainly, something endearing about Kim Dotcom's attitude. He acts like a man who finds his own obesity hilarious. His relationship to pop culture gives him a childlike appeal. (He once made himself the main character in a seminal flash-animation film that centered on the cartoonish murder of Bill Gates. He named his animated alter ego Richard Kimball, the wrongly accused hero from *The Fugitive*.) Sometimes it seems like he can't possibly be serious. (After his arrest, he recorded an anti-copyright ABBA-like pop song titled "Mr. President" in which he directly compares himself to Martin Luther King.) In general, Americans enjoy the idea of computer hackers and prefer to imagine them as precocious elves. (Somehow, the touchstone for how hackers behave is still based on Matthew Broderick's performance in the 1983 film *WarGames*.) Dotcom is arrogant, but not unlikable; at the highest possible level, being an IT guy is vaguely cool. Yet his underlying message is troubling. He starts by arguing, "Change is good," which is only a semi-defensible position to begin with. But that evolves into "Change will happen whether you like it or not." He uses phrases like *"The law of human nature is to communicate more efficiently,"* which makes it seem like he's proposing something natural and obvious. But all he's really proposing is the business model for his own company (which might not be diabolical, but certainly isn't altruistic). He's trying to initiate an era when content is free and content providers make all the money, but he still wants to frame it like a more grassroots system (*"The people of the Internet will unite"*). Would his espoused structure actually be better? I don't think it's possible to know. But I do know that any argument attacking Dotcom will come from a position of sad technological inferiority. It will seem unsophisticated and antediluvian. It's easier to just embrace Dotcom's viewpoint, even if it's self-serving and unfair; about a year after the initial raid, he launched another sharing service (this time simply called MEGA) that utilizes cloud technology. I suspect it will succeed. He is, in many ways, the most depressing kind of villain: the kind we *must* agree with in order to stay competitive. The only other option is being trampled.

* * *

> There is a view that one should never be permitted to be criticized for being—possibly, even in the future—engaged in a contributory act that might be immoral. And that type of arse covering is more important than saving people's lives. That it is better to let 1000 people die than risk going to save them and possibly running over someone on the way. And that is something I find philosophically repugnant.

These are the words of Julian Assange, the founder of the website WikiLeaks and the most archetypically villainlike villain of the Internet age. His appearance is so Aryan that it seems like he was engineered by the kind of scientist who ends up hiding in Argentina. I assume Assange can laugh, but I have no proof. He's truly a worldwide irritant: Assange has been accused of sexually assaulting two women in Sweden, applied for political asylum in Ecuador, and had a Canadian academic call for his assassination. His brilliance is impolite and self-defined. There is no one else like him; he is truly a New Thing.

If you know what WikiLeaks is, feel free to skip this paragraph. (I'm not going to outline anything you don't already know, nor am I going to take a strong position on its merits or flaws, nor have I seen the yet-to-be released film *The Fifth Estate* starring sexy British weirdo Benedict Cumberbatch in the lead role.) If you don't know anything about it, here's a 230-word description: WikiLeaks is a website that publishes classified, present-tense documents from anonymous sources. The site's abiding premise is that the upside of absolute transparency is greater than the potential downside of publicly dumping sensitive information that might theoretically cause damage. The first noteworthy WikiLeaks release was some 2007 footage of a U.S. Apache helicopter killing an Iraqi journalist in Afghanistan (people generally viewed this release positively). The most discussed incident was an avalanche of "diplomatic cables" that went up in 2011; essentially, these were private correspondences American diplomats had exchanged among themselves. Most of these exchanges were more gossipy than meaningful, but it made some high-profile Americans seem crazy and facile. [It also created the impression that WikiLeaks cannot be controlled or regulated, which seemed scarier than the documents themselves.] That same year, WikiLeaks released seventy-five thousand U.S. military documents that came to be known as the Afghan War Diary. The Pentagon wasn't exactly stoked about this. Obviously, the details of all these fiascoes can be found more comprehensively elsewhere. But the takeaway is this: A very confident Australian (Assange) who's fixated on the problematic

politics of one country (the United States) has created a way to publish information about that country that would have previously remained hidden (sometimes for valid reasons and sometimes due to corruption). It is journalism that attacks journalism, which is an extremely interesting topic to journalists.

Supporters of WikiLeaks believe it receives the same kind of unjust, reactionary criticism that was once lobbed at the Pentagon Papers (the Pentagon Papers were a classified overview of U.S. military involvement in the Vietnam War, published by the *New York Times* in 1971). Those who are against WikiLeaks counter this argument by noting that the Pentagon Papers were vetted by a news organization and only involved defunct military actions that were at least four years old (the study examined activities only through the year 1967). It's worth noting that the principal whistleblower in the Pentagon Papers (former U.S. military analyst Daniel Ellsberg) has requested a presidential pardon for the principle whistleblower in the WikiLeaks controversy, former U.S. soldier Bradley Manning. I have my own views on this topic, but they're contradictory and unimportant. What intrigues me more is Assange's quote at the top of this section: His statement either confronts (and obliterates) the problem I'm trying to describe, or it simply *is* the problem (described succinctly and expressed with monotone glee).

Assange comes at the media from a bottom-line, non-theoretical, the-ends-justify-the-means perspective that was (perhaps not so coincidentally) first described in Machiavelli's *The Prince*. He's arguing that people are too obsessed with the arcane ethics of print journalism, and he's willing to accept that an action that hurts one person is justified if it helps a hundred or a thousand or ten thousand others. It's an old problem. Perhaps the clearest metaphor for how much this disturbs people is the classic hypothetical of the runaway trolley car: Imagine you are operating a trolley car whose brakes have malfunctioned. You are flying down the tracks at an obscene speed. Up ahead, you see five workers on the track, unaware that this trolley is bearing down on them; if you continue on your current path, the trolley will kill them all. But then you notice an alternate track that will allow you to avoid colliding with the five workers. The only downside is that if you turn onto this alternate route, you will kill a different innocent person (but only one). Do you switch to the alternate track and kill one person in order to save five? [The folks usually credited with the creation and popularization of this dilemma are Philippa Foot and Judith Jarvis Thomson, but I'm roughly paraphrasing how it's described in Michael Sandel's wonderful book *Justice*.]

When you pose this question to any normal reader, they almost always say yes. It seems insane to kill five people instead of one. But that's not the true question; that's just the introduction. The real question is this: Let's say you're *not* operating the runaway trolley. Let's say you're not the conductor. Let's propose that you're just watching this event from a bridge above the track. You realize this runaway trolley is going to kill five people. You notice another person is watching this event alongside you—an extremely obese man. It dawns on you that if you push this man onto the track below, it will derail the trolley. Here again, you are killing one man in order to save five. Do you push the fat man off the bridge?

This second scenario always troubles people more: The most common answer tends to be, "I know these things are basically the same, but I could never push a man to his death." The reason people feel different is due to how the two scenarios position the decision maker. In the first problem, the decision maker is accepting the existing conditions and trying to choose whatever solution hurts the fewest individuals. In the second problem, the decision maker is injecting himself into the situation and taking on the responsibility of the outcome. The first scenario is a reaction. The second is a self-directed choice. What bothers people about WikiLeaks is that it creates a world in which the second scenario is happening constantly, and what bothers people about Assange is the way he makes that choice seem so stupidly self-evident.

Assange's belief is that everyone would be better off if all information was equally (and immediately) available. His critics say, "That's irresponsible. If you just release information—and particularly military information—without considering its sensitivity, someone will get killed." And that's probably true. If WikiLeaks continues in its current iteration, I'm sure it will (eventually) contribute to someone's death. But Assange makes us consider the larger value of that troubling possibility. What if the relentless release of classified information makes every nation less willing to conduct questionable military actions? Will this force all society to become more honest (and wouldn't that future reality be worth the loss of a hundred innocent people in the present)? Or would it actually make things worse? Will the fear of exposure simply prompt political figures to resist creating any paper trail at all? Will *everything* become hidden? I really have no idea. No one does, and that's the discomfort: We don't know if the old way is better (or worse) than the new way. But Assange does not let us choose. He possesses a sweeping technological advantage, and he knows that released information cannot be retracted. He can make us accept his philosophy against our will. Once a document is released, how we feel about the nature of its existence becomes meaningless; it's instantaneously absorbed into the media bloodstream as pure content. This is why Assange can make an argument that openly advocates actions that (in his words) "might be immoral." Those actions are going to happen anyway, so he doesn't have to pretend that they contradict the way we've always viewed morality. He doesn't have to convince us he's right, because our thoughts don't matter. His view of *everything* is like Perez Hilton's view of gossip or Kim Dotcom's view of entertainment: He believes everything longs to be free. And he will make that happen, because he knows how to do it and we don't know how to stop him. He's already beaten everybody. It was never close.

"I AM PERPLEXED"

[THIS IS WHY, THIS IS WHY,

THIS IS WHY THEY HATE YOU]

It was a good question that seemed like a bad question: An unsmiling nineteen-year-old man asked me why he hated Fred Durst. He did not ask me if I hated Fred Durst; he asked me why he hated Fred Durst. I said, "Isn't that a question I should be asking you?" He said, "No, I want *you* to tell *me*." I asked if this was supposed to be a guessing game. He said, "No, I don't know the answer. Tell me the answer."

I said, "Well, you probably hate the music of Limp Bizkit [Durst's despised, platinum-selling rap-rock band], so you unconsciously direct that vitriol at the person singing the lyrics."

"No," he replied. "The music is okay. I don't listen to it, but it's not terrible. That song 'Break Stuff' is funny. But I still hate Fred Durst. Explain this to me. Explain why I hate him."

I started telling a story about something that happened when I worked at *Spin* magazine in 2004: The art department had received a paparazzi photo of Durst, taken at the premiere of the Tarantino film *Kill Bill: Volume 2*. Durst was wearing a T-shirt promoting the Smiths, the defunct British pop band fronted by Morrissey and defined by their fey, alienated aesthetic. Everyone in the office immediately made the same joke. "Oh, look—Fred Durst wants to go back to high school so he can kick his own ass." Maybe this is the reason, I argued. Maybe it's the fact that Durst seems insincere about both the menacing persona he projects in Limp Bizkit and the thoughtful artistic persona he projects as a celebrity.

"No, not really," said the nineteen-year-old. "I mean, aren't the Smiths supposed to be good? Why would that make me hate him? Shouldn't that make me like him?"

He had a point (and I still did not). I attempted to make a more academic argument about how the Limp Bizkit song "Nookie" was misogynist for suggesting that the protagonist's ex-girlfriend should inject a cookie into her vagina (or maybe that she should somehow fold her vagina into her rectum—the specific lyrics have never been clear). However, I quit halfway through my lecture. Even as I was talking, I could instantly imagine how this kid would respond. He'd probably say, "But Biggie Smalls has a song about kidnapping the teenage daughter of a federal prosecutor and tying her up in a Brooklyn basement, and everybody still loves him. The Rolling Stones song 'Under My Thumb' is so sexist that Rush Limbaugh was fired from his college radio job for playing it too much, and they're the most popular band in the history of the world. James Taylor seems like the worst husband of the seventies. James Brown literally punched women in the face. How is Fred Durst worse for wearing a backwards baseball cap and singing about cookies and birth canals?"

I gave up.

"I don't know," I slowly concluded. "Maybe you don't actually hate him. Maybe you just think you do. Maybe you secretly love him, and that's the thing that bothers you."

"No," he said. "I hate Fred Durst. That's the one thing I know for sure."

"But how can you be certain?" I asked.

He looked at me like I was crazy, and then he walked away.

They Hate You Because You Hate Yourself. In 2002, the Friars Club of New York City sponsored a roast for Chevy Chase. It was subsequently aired on Comedy Central, but only once—the participants were so cruel that it didn't feel funny. Making matters worse was a general lack of participation from the many major stars Chase worked with throughout his career, thereby suggesting that people hate Chevy Chase so much they wouldn't even show up to ridicule him. The book *Live From New York,* a comprehensive oral history of *Saturday Night Live,* is littered with people taking direct and veiled shots at Chase, most memorably through a description of a fistfight between Chevy and Bill Murray that concluded with Murray spitting the epithet, "Medium talent." This remains the greatest possible insult you can throw at any creative person: It suggests that the individual is both overrated and underachieving at the same time.

Chase's confrontation with Murray happened backstage at *SNL* in 1978, long before the public knew much about who these people really were; as such, the first wave of Chevy Haters were more exasperated by his personality than his perception. The conventional wisdom is that the early *SNL* performers disliked Chase because of a) their jealousy and b) his arrogance and sexism. When he returned to guest-host the program in 1985, he was described by cast members as a "monster" who wanted to do material considerably darker than the show's traditionally unadventurous counterculture posturing (for example, he wanted to do a skit about AIDS). Chase remains a problematic genius that other problematic geniuses despise (most notably *Community* creator Dan Harmon, who worked with him for three seasons before publicly declaring him an asshole). He's possibly just a standard jerk, unless every single person in Hollywood is lying. But there's something deeper here; there's something about Chevy Chase's view *of himself* that makes him villainous to people who will never meet him and have no reason to feel anything personal: He is a man who consciously risks nothing, seemingly as punishment for whatever it is he believes he is not.

Virtually all funny people have a subterranean desire to be

taken seriously. Nobody can explain why this happens, but funny people understand it intuitively. This is true for all of Chevy's peers: His nemesis Murray pursued that goal once as a young man (1984's *The Razor's Edge*) and compulsively as an older one (2005's *Broken Flowers*, 2009's *Get Low*, 2012's *Hyde Park on the Hudson*). At the height of his comedic powers, Steve Martin starred in the 1981 musical *Pennies from Heaven*. Dan Aykroyd was in *Driving Miss Daisy*. John Belushi made *Continental Divide* and played it straight. Tom Hanks got serious with *Philadelphia* and eventually dominated the seriousness field. Jim Carrey is still trying. Robin Williams spent half his life making this transition, eventually winning an Oscar for *Good Will Hunting*; Eddie Murphy made his attempt with *Dreamgirls* but only got the Golden Globe. It's something all mainstream comedians inevitably attempt—but not Chevy Chase. He has never taken a serious role (supposedly, the closest he ever came was turning down Richard Gere's role in *American Gigolo*). What makes this especially strange is how natural Chase would have been as a leading man: Of all the seventies comedians, he was the most classically handsome and the least emotively manic. He could have killed any role that required understatement; deadpan is his default setting. But this did not intrigue him. For the most part, he never tries to act at all. He just plays himself as a golfer (or as a detective, or as a bad father, or as an invisible man, or as whatever). When described as a professional worldview, that artistic choice seems admirable: It sounds less fake, less needy, and more self-aware. But that's not how it comes across. It's important not to take oneself too seriously, but Chevy refused to take himself seriously *at all*. It was as if he saw his own career as too ridiculous to care about. And something about that attitude slowly insults people. They feel as if the performer is mocking their support for his art, which even the performer views as meaningless. The fear with Chevy Chase is that every role is just another manifestation of "the Real Chevy"—that all these identical characters reflect the person he truly is, and that all his alleged arrogance is the product of believing he's the only person smart enough to recognize how *everything* is a clumsy joke, including love and death and unedited emotion. He's the only person smart enough not to care about anything. That's what he means when he says, "I'm Chevy Chase, and you're not." It's not something he's happy about.

I see all of Chevy's worst qualities in myself. But none of his good ones.

They hate you because you always need to be right. And ultimately, Howard Cosell was (not always in the specific, but usually in the abstract). Since his death in 1995, Cosell's reputation as a broadcaster has exponentially increased; he is now regarded almost as highly as he incessantly insisted he deserved. If you list the titans of sports media, he's always in the top five and often number one, depending on the degree to which you see "polarization" as an indication of import. But even that designation is imperfect, since "polarization" suggests there were two equal, diametrically opposed views of Howard Cosell. This is not really how it was: He was hated with uniformity. During the apex of his reign, troglodytes would go to bars and drunkenly throw bricks at TV sets during *Monday Night Football* telecasts (a company later manufactured Styrofoam bricks so that people could do this at home without damaging the family Sylvania). Dumb people hated Cosell for talking like the lawyer that he was, but smart people hated him, too. They hated him for being shallow and self-absorbed. Historian David Halberstam called him "the classic modern telecelebrity," which—considering the source—was far more insulting than it might appear on the surface.

The entire spectrum of these insults bothered Cosell. He saw all criticisms as equal. All his professional colleagues have at least one story of Cosell hopelessly railing against some random snipe from a fifth-tier newspaper columnist living in a town he'd never deign to visit—had Howard lived in the age of Google Alert, he might have stroked out before turning fifty. But not all of those snipes were minor: People threatened to bomb stadiums where he was scheduled to announce meaningless football games. It would have been easy to feel sympathy for him were it not for his strident inability to fake humility: "There's one thing about this business [of broadcasting]," he said in 1967. "There is no place in it for talent. That's why I don't belong. I lack sufficient mediocrity."

Because the Internet cannot disappear, there will always be a searchable archive for the gallons of haterade dumped upon twenty-first century sportscasters: Jay Mariotti, Skip Bayless, Joe Morgan, Chris Berman. Their eviscerations are constant and crude. Yet the composite distaste for all those figures is just a fraction of the pathological, unpublished hate directed at Cosell throughout the 1970s. The proof of that math will fade over time, simply because the main detritus will end up being the nice things about his life: his cameo in Woody Allen's *Bananas,* his political support for Muhammad Ali, and the singularity of his nasal delivery ("Down goes Frazier! Down goes Frazier!"). In this way, Howard prevailed; it's hard to imagine people who still hate Cosell today or what their motive would be. And this is too bad. It's too bad because that hatred was the most important thing about him. It *made him* important. He was, for more than a decade, the conduit through which working-class American males wrestled with the concept of anti-intellectualism. He was the single best argument for and against that particular mind-set. Everything he said had multiple meanings, most of which had nothing to do with sport. He usually mattered more than the subjects he covered. I remember watching a *Monday Night Football* game with my elderly uncle, who casually referred to Cosell as "a New York Jew." The revelation blew my mind. "How does my uncle know that Howard Cosell is Jewish?" my nine-year-old self wondered silently. "Does he talk about his religious views at halftime?" In 1982, Cosell covered a brutal heavyweight boxing match between Larry Holmes and Randall "Tex" Cobb; for fifteen rounds, Holmes pummeled the outclassed Cobb so relentlessly that Cosell vowed to never announce another fight. It was an ethical decision based on justifiable criteria, but it made him look buffoonish to the common man: The still-healing Cobb quipped that he'd let Holmes punch him in the face for another fifteen rounds if Howard promised to quit covering football, too.

It never mattered if Cosell was lecturing on a subject he understood deeply (such as Ali's constitutional rights as a pacifist) or something he did not understand at all (like the strategic nuances of baseball). His reasoning was always circular: "What I'm saying is true because I am the person saying it." Of course, Cosell would have never expressed anything that clearly: "The veracity of my pellucid acumen is validated not by the words alone, but by the indomitable vanguard who uttered them at their inception." This was his thing, as much as anything else—the obfuscation of language (which, I suppose, I am equally guilty of, particularly when I use words like *obfuscation*). But that habit meant something profound when placed in the context of a football game or a boxing match. If you hated Cosell, it seemed like he was trying to complicate something visceral in order to compensate for his own weakness; if you were charmed by Cosell, you still got the sense he was condescending to his subject in order to showcase his obvious superiority. Nobody thought Howard Cosell was only okay. The very smart believed he was fake smart; the semismart thought he was too smart for his own good; the not-so-smart assumed he was an idiot (and sometimes they were right, which is why all of those opinions mattered to Howard equally).

I see all of Cosell's worst qualities in myself. But none of his good ones.

They hate you because you went all the way. It does not seem like photographs of Aleister Crowley should exist. Paintings? Sure. But not photos. He seems like a creature who should have lived long ago, before cameras, within whatever fictional time frame *Advanced Dungeons & Dragons* is supposed to be set. Like most males of my generation, I first learned of Crowley (and continue to mispronounce his name) thanks to the organ-driven Ozzy Osbourne song "Mr. Crowley." Years later, I was shocked to discover that Aleister's 1947 death occurred just twelve months before Ozzy's birth; had Crowley taken better care of his lungs, the two men could have existed simultaneously. The deviant pair are linked forever; a 2003 article in the *Journal of Religion and Popular Culture* directly compared their influence on the prevalent view of faux Satanism. ["Though their deepest motives are different," author Christopher M. Moreman notes, "they share the need for fame, both going to extremes to attain it. This selfish need is couched in different forms by both men, one actively seeking to change society despite the people, with the other seeking only to please the people in the midst of a society-changing movement."] The title of Crowley's best novel (*Diary of a Drug Fiend*) is thematically transposable with the title of Osbourne's second solo album (*Diary of a Madman*). At this point in history, both are representations of cartoonish evil, and Ozzy is far more famous. But this will not be the case in three hundred years; in three hundred years, Osbourne will be mostly forgotten, whereas Crowley will occupy the same cultural space he does today. Which is to say he will always be remembered as the person who put *the most effort* into being recognized as evil.

Had Crowley bitten the head off a bat or pissed on the walls of the Alamo, it would barely qualify as memorable. Relatively speaking, both acts would be footnotes within a much stranger career. As a young British boy in the late nineteenth century, Crowley killed the same cat nine different ways, just to find out if cats really had nine lives. This, as much as anything, portends how his mind would always work. He wasn't insane. He was perverse. Raised in affluence as a Quaker, Crowley was eleven when his father died from tongue cancer. This is how he recounted the death in his journal: "I had some respect, but no love, for my father. And from the moment of his funeral, I entered a new phase of development, the main feature of which was nonconformity . . . it was around this time that I began to rebel and fantasize about torture and blood, often imagining myself being hurt and in agony." At first blush, this sounds like teen posturing; it reads like something an erudite Ronnie James Dio fan would write in sophomore English. But Crowley goes further than the abnormal teenager, which is precisely what makes him Crowley. "Of course, just as any young boy, my vivid imagination also began to turn to the opposite sex. But in particular, I had visions of being degraded and suffering at the hands of wicked women." This is, obviously, a peculiar desire. But Crowley goes further still, later writing, "Pleasure as such has never attracted me. It must be spiced by moral satisfaction." In other words, he felt all the physical urges for sex, but needed sex to be both degrading and—somehow—ethically rewarding. He was like a druggier L. Ron Hubbard: He just sort of created an ever-devolving belief system as he marched through life, reverse-engineering his intellectual morality to fit whatever new awful decision he happened to make. Two of his central creeds were a) never make claims that cannot be proven and b) never pretend to be something you are not. This is actually excellent advice, although horribly impractical for a pansexual magick user who once tried to kill a personal rival with mind bullets.

So what did Aleister Crowley *do*, really? This is always the key question. He was a writer (he saw himself as Oscar Wilde's dark, twisted fantasy) and he was a "real" magician (in order to avoid pickpockets in India, he claims to have rendered himself invisible). He was a mountaineer (Crowley tried to climb K2 in 1902 and nearly succeeded) and a general spouter of immoderate aphorisms ("Do what thou wilt shall be the whole of the Law"). He was born rich but wasted every penny; by 1924 he was living in poverty in France. Some people think he was a World War II spy (unlikely). Some believe he's the biological grandfather of George

W. Bush (equally unlikely, but not totally implausible—Aleister did party with the mother of W's mother, Pauline Pierce, the year before she gave birth to a baby girl who'd become Barbara Bush). I suppose a Crowley apologist would argue he "modernized" the concept of magic and mysticism in 1912 with two books, *Magick (Book 4)* and *The Book of Lies,* thus forging the foundation for the Thelema and Wiccan religions. But those achievements strike me as just slightly less than totally goofy. The main thing Aleister Crowley did was be himself, which is why he was so good at it. His single-minded focus on being terrible remains unchallenged. And this was not a situation like N.W.A or the Oakland Raiders, where the perception of badness was supposed to inform the art; this was a situation where the badness had to be real. The badness *was* the art. He literally had to eat all the drugs and oppose the concept of nature and sharpen his incisors into fangs and throw his mother-in-law down a flight of stairs. Certainly, a lot of what we "know" about Crowley is based in false mythology (even during his own lifetime, there was a rumor that he ate two employees on a mountain-climbing expedition). But what's crazier is that Crowley desperately wanted these rumors to be true. Near the end of his life, he boasted about potentially inspiring *Mein Kampf* by mailing a young Adolf Hitler a copy of his seminal work *The Book of the Law.* "Before Hitler was," said the Yoda-like Crowley, "I am." This would be akin to Ozzy retroactively changing the title of his song "Suicide Solution" to "Suicide Is the Best Possible Solution for Everyone, Even if Your Life Is Awesome and You Want to Live."

It's probably not surprising that my personal interest in Crowley was—for many years—exclusively tied to his accidental relationship with heavy rock music and my obsession with all the British artists he mesmerized (as opposed to my staunch lack of interest in the one American non-artist who actually fulfilled his promise—G. G. Allin). By far the most intimately remembered detail of Crowley's legacy is that Led Zeppelin mastermind

Jimmy Page purchased the dead occultist's Boleskine mansion on the shore of Loch Ness. It was here that the pale guitarist would sit in the dark, shoot heroin, and think about the devil. It was a real Crowley-like move on Page's behalf: Let me live in the home of the sickest person I can think of and try to get sicker. "Although I don't agree with everything he said, he was a visionary," Page is quoted as saying in *Tangents Within a Framework,* a book first published in 1983. "I don't particularly want to go into it, because it's a personal thing and isn't in relation to anything I do as a musician, apart that I've employed his system into my own day-to-day life." I'm not sure how this is supposed to be taken, unless it means Page cast a spell on whoever played bass on Kingdom Come's second record. Today, Page claims his interest in Crowley was blown out of proportion (and I think he feels a little dumb about buying that mansion). But I do know this: It still means something to care about Aleister Crowley. It's code. It's like carrying a gun into a maternity ward; it means your superficial sympathies fall with the opposite of whatever you were taught to believe. One Christmas, a caustic friend gave me an audio collection of Crowley's "music," which includes recorded chanting from Mr. Crowley himself. It doesn't sound like anything remotely good (every single track is super boring, and I can't make out a word of whatever he's saying). But I have other (generally nonreligious) friends who refuse to let me play this CD in their presence, even for scholastic purposes. They do not want to hear it. Do they honestly fear something evil will happen? No. That's not part of their belief system. But it doesn't seem worth the gamble, and it never will. I mean, why risk it? Who knows with this guy, really?

I see all of Crowley's worst qualities in myself. But none of the good ones.

[Actually, that's not true at all.]

I was watching a football game. It was the playoffs. It was third down. Pierre Garçon ran a curl pattern, and Peyton Manning missed him. The Colts had to punt, and the Jets went on to win 17–16. In retrospect, that third-down pass play didn't matter at all. But at the time it mattered enough for me to spontaneously look at the Internet on my phone, because (for reasons I'll never understand) I wanted to see what other people thought about Peyton Manning missing Pierre Garçon on a curl pattern. However, no one on Twitter was Tweeting about this third-down play; I suppose a few people were, somewhere, but those dissidents were being suffocated by a different problem that was more important and less clear.

It was like watching the world unravel in real time. But then it raveled back.

There had been a shooting in Arizona. I hadn't heard the news, but I could piece it together, 140 characters at a time: Someone had appeared in the parking lot of a Tucson Safeway and shot nineteen people. The principal target was U.S. Representative Gabrielle Giffords, who was shot in the head at point-blank range (and *target* would become the operative word here, at least for twenty-four to forty-eight hours). So now I'm reading about murder on my phone and following NFL football on my TV. My eyes are toggling between the two present-tense realities, and I'm not truly concentrating on either. But I start to notice a pattern on my phone; I start to see Sarah Palin's name in half the posts I scroll past. And then the entire tone of Twitter shifts: People are still using words like *tragedy,* but the tenor in which they employ that word borders on gleeful. I was still having a hard time figuring out precisely what had happened in Tucson, but I started to sense that Palin's career as a public figure was on the verge of ending (even if I couldn't isolate why).

Now, I'm an apolitical person (which I realize is its own kind of misleading political posture, but I think you know what I mean). I do not have conventional political affiliations. I follow presidential elections the same way I follow the NFL playoffs: obsessively and dispassionately. But Sarah Palin was (and is) a real problem. Her nomination for vice president in 2008 represents the most desperate inclinations of the Republican Party. In two hundred years, I suspect historians will use Palin as an example of how insane America became in the decade following the destruction of the World Trade Center, and her origin story will seem as extraterrestrial and eccentric as Abe Lincoln jumping out of a window to undermine a voting quorum in 1840. This was not totally her fault, but it was mostly her fault. Yet, still . . . what did Palin possibly have to do with the shooting of Giffords (and why was everyone on Twitter so certain she was culpable)? I had no idea. My initial theory was that she must have come forward and *supported* the assassination attempt, which struck me as both totally unthinkable and marginally plausible. This was what I wondered while the Jets' Nick Folk kicked a thirty-two-yard field goal to beat the Colts. Thirty seconds after the kick, I walked into my office and started reading about the Tucson shooting (in complete sentences), focused on why this event was prompting so many people to pretend they were sad about a situation that was clearly making them euphoric.

They were euphoric about a map.

It seems there was a map of the United States displayed on the Internet, designed by Palin (or someone who worked for her) in March of 2010, seven months before that year's midterm elections. The site was called Take Back the 20, and it specified the twenty congressional Democrats that Palin hoped would lose in November. The twenty were geographically pinpointed with the crosshairs of a gun scope, sort of like a James Bond poster or the cover of a Public Enemy album (and intended to be taken more seriously than the former but less so than the latter). One of the crosshairs was fixed on Giffords. The subsequent "logic path" was predictable: The shooter was obviously a fanatical Palin supporter who took the map literally, which means the true killer was Palin. The secondary logic path was more nuanced, but only slightly: Perhaps the person wasn't *literally* killing Giffords on

Palin's behalf, but the "rhetoric" advocated by Palin supported a culture where liberal politicians might get shot. Palin activists responded by taking the map off the Internet. They claimed the crosshairs did not represent a gun but rather the scope of a road surveyor; this immediately made them seem ten times guiltier and one hundred times less reasonable. But then—first gradually, and then overwhelmingly—the story changed. The gunman was a conspiracy-driven schizophrenic named Jared Loughner who'd been obsessed with Giffords for three years. (He was still outraged over her unwillingness to sufficiently answer the following question at a 2007 political event: "What is government if words have no meaning?") To me, this made the story far more compelling. But the rest of the country disagreed; three weeks after the shooting, the story had essentially disappeared from the American news cycle (which would never have happened if Loughner had actually been motivated by Palin's map). It seemed crazy to direct vitriol at Loughner, because *he* was crazy. Loughner was perceived as more pathetic than sinister, and you can't hate the pathetic (because that makes *you* pathetic). There was ultimately nothing to take away from this story, beyond the fact that a) crazy people do crazy things, and b) it's easy to get guns in Arizona.

But I want to go back to the moment just after the football game ended.

I want to return to the moment before we knew who Loughner was; I want to reopen the window of time when the center of the story was Palin (and nobody knew how much responsibility needed to be dumped on her Neiman Marcus shoulder pads). It seemed like a critical moment for democracy. Was Palin truly finished? She had already become a political nonfactor, but now she might be a cultural nonfactor; if she had any tangible connection to the assassination of a rival politician, there would be no way for her to recover. There would be no comeback. And part of me knew this might be good for the country. Intellectually, I understood why the metaphorical elimination of Palin might be better for the world at large. But I *felt* something else: sympathy. (And since feelings are merely uncontained thoughts, I suppose I was thinking it, too.) I began rooting for Sarah Palin. I wanted all the bozos on my Twitter feed to be wrong. I empathized with her situation, I believed she'd been unfairly railroaded, and I couldn't decide if the creation of that map was mildly problematic or completely irrelevant. I started to see the world from her perspective, which was jarring and intriguing. I still saw her as a problem, but that evening was absolutely the most I ever liked her.

Which made me wonder: Why do I always want to turn the bad guy into the good guy? Why does this make me feel better?

They hate you because you don't hate anyone, even when you should.

CRIME AND PUNISHMENT
(OR THE LACK THEREOF)

I had to take a lot of psychological tests. These tests asked certain questions. One of the questions was, "When you walk into a room, do you think everybody's looking at you?" *Yes!* "When you walk into a room, do you feel people are talking about you?" *Yeah, I do.* Now, if a normal person says "yes" to those questions, they have some kind of complex. They have some kind of problem. But (for me), it's true. I know when I walk into a room, people are looking at me. I know when I walk into a restaurant, people are talking about me.

—O. J. Simpson, telling the truth

I didn't really seek attention. I just wanted to play the game well and go home.

—Kareem Abdul-Jabbar,
being honest

It's unfair to write this, but I'm going to do it anyway: Kareem Abdul-Jabbar and O. J. Simpson have a lot in common. We don't normally lump them together, because certain key contrasts are tricky—for example, one man is a Muslim intellectual and the other more or less decapitated his ex-wife. This is more than a significant detail. But let's think about that specific dissonance last. Before we examine what makes them different, here's what makes them similar . . .

1) Both are known by names that do not reflect their original identities. Abdul-Jabbar was born Lew Alcindor, which he changed for religious reasons; Simpson was born "Orenthal James" but chose to go by his initials for simplicity and panache.

2) Both attended college in Los Angeles during a period of massive social upheaval: Abdul-Jabbar arrived at UCLA in 1965, while Simpson showed up at USC in 1967.

3) Both were culturally defined by their response to identity politics. Jabbar refused to participate in the '68 Olympics in accordance with the black power movement and has recalled an "antiwhite" phase he explored during high school; Simpson is generally viewed as the first black athlete who was able to break into the white world of advertising endorsements on a national scale.

4) Both had high-profile relationships with white women (and were unjustly criticized for it).

5) Both began their professional careers in small markets (Abdul-Jabbar in Milwaukee, Simpson in Buffalo) and both finished on the West Coast (L.A. and San Francisco).

6) Both were the premier superstars of their respective sports throughout the 1970s. This is unquestionably true for Abdul-Jabbar, the winner of six NBA MVPs from 1971 to 1980. It's a more debatable designation for Simpson, but he was absolutely the best running back in an era dominated by the running game.

7) Both played at least one season longer than they should have.

8) Both became actors who are best remembered for supporting roles in absurdist, farcical comedies directed by David
Zucker (Kareem in *Airplane!*, O.J. in the *Naked Gun* series).

9) Both are—to wildly varying degrees—vilified figures. One
was vilified slowly, for reasons that were shallow and often
specious. The other was vilified suddenly and dramatically,
in a way history will never forget. But they each illustrate
something uncomfortable about the relationship between
those who are famous and those who consume fame. There
is a collective expectation that celebrities—and especially
black celebrities—will calibrate their relationship to the
public within a specific window of acceptable exposure.
They will not be too private or too public. The size of the
window is different for every person, but it always (somehow) exists. And if a celebrity drifts outside that space—in
either direction, and for any purpose—that (somehow) validates whatever people believed about them in the first place.

I am not, in any way, trying to argue that the "unpopularity" of
O. J. Simpson is mainly a reflection of his media persona. This
would be like claiming Christianity became popular because people trust beards. The reason Simpson is despised is because virtually all rational humans believe he brutally murdered his ex-wife
Nicole Brown and a handsome waiter named Ronald Goldman
(who happened to be at Brown's home when the killer showed up
on the evening of June 12, 1994). After a trial that lasted almost a
year, Simpson was found not guilty by a jury of his peers. It's still
not totally clear how this happened. The best argument is that the
Los Angeles Police Department wrecked the prosecution's case
by attempting to frame an already guilty man. Another strong
possibility is that the prosecuting attorneys were amazingly inept
and choked under the pressure. Still another theory suggests that
the jury was unconsciously equalizing centuries of racial unfair-

ness by allowing the black Simpson to walk for a crime he clearly committed; a more insulting (but not impossible) hypothesis is that the members of the jury were not educated enough to understand the magnitude of the DNA evidence. There is, I suppose, the infinitesimal possibility that Simpson actually *was* innocent, and that the twelve members of the jury are the only twelve Americans who saw this case devoid of bias; a handful of rogue contrarians have made the argument that the murders were actually committed by O.J.'s son Jason, which is slightly less ridiculous than it sounds (but only slightly).

I'm not going to try and reprove the state's case against Simpson, because no person needs that. What I'm interested in is the period after Simpson's acquittal, considered from the (fictional) perspective of an honest, wrongly persecuted O.J. It necessitates an ethical question that is rarely asked: If you were wrongly accused of murder and found not guilty, how would you live the rest of your life, particularly if everyone in the world still believed you were the murderer?

"I advised him, and many people advised him, to do what Claus von Bülow did after he was acquitted [of trying to kill his wife]: disappear from the public view." These are the words of Alan Dershowitz, von Bülow's appellate lawyer in 1984 and an advisor to Simpson's defense team. He said these words in a documentary titled *O.J.: Monster or Myth?*, an ostensibly pro-Simpson film that makes O.J. seem extra guilty. "Of course, O. J. Simpson never followed that advice," Dershowitz continued. "On the night of the acquittal, he called in to *The Larry King Show*."

Because Simpson has always seemed so bombastically culpable, it's impossible to view his post-trial profile in any other way. But for a moment, let's pretend: Let's pretend that you are O.J. and that you are innocent. Let's pretend that someone you once loved was murdered, and every coherent person in the world assumed you were the killer. Let's pretend you were acquitted in a trial that everyone watched on television, so the espoused wrongheadedness of the outcome is culturally omnipresent. Let's also pretend your skin color is a central aspect of the conversation, and that you've already been famous for twenty-five years before any of this had happened, and that Joni Mitchell has written a song about you (sarcastically titled "Not to Blame") that doubles as a backhanded condemnation of Jackson Browne's relationship with Daryl Hannah.

How would you live the rest of your life?

There are three options:

- The first option would be to leave the country and live as an exile in someplace like Australia or France. At first, this will seem like the smart move. It almost feels like the obvious move. But it has some glaring downsides. On a practical level, it would mean abandoning or uprooting your children (who, in theory, would now need you more than ever). Despite being found not guilty in the criminal trial, you would still need to return to the U.S. for the inevitable civil trial. But these are the small problems. The larger problems are more metaphoric. If you're innocent, leaving a country you love makes it seem like you're imprisoning yourself. It's like self-imposing a penalty for a crime you did not commit. More important, fleeing the country as an innocent person *makes you seem guilty.* One assumes part of Alan Dershowitz's advisement to Simpson was based on the fact that Dershowitz never believed his client hadn't committed the crime he was acquitted of.

- A second option would be to exit public life while remaining in America. This feels like a reasonable tactic. Yet it would be virtually hopeless, even in the bygone twentieth century. Simpson had been appearing on television commercials for over twenty years (most notably for Hertz rent-a-car) when he suddenly found himself featured on multiple TV networks, all day long, for over a year. This would not be a situation like J. D. Salinger, where only weirdos wanted to find you; you'd be hunted by tabloids on a daily basis (particularly if you were putting sincere effort into being unseen, thus making every image even more valuable). You also have to consider how unnatural this shift would feel to a person of O.J.'s stature; for most of his life, being famous was the best part of who he was. It was the intangible reward for being fast and difficult to tackle and socially intelligent; it granted him access to a tier of society that would have normally shut him out, and it allowed him to date women who looked like Nicole Brown.

• The third option—and the one Simpson selected—was to actually live like the innocent person he portrayed himself to be. He actively looked for publicity and tried to monetize his experience (which seems callous, but—were he truly innocent—not undeserved). He played a shitload of golf. He went to all the Los Angeles restaurants he'd missed when he was in jail. He did not show any remorse, based on the principle that there was nothing for him to feel remorseful about; he did not express a preponderance of grief over the death of his ex-wife, but she'd now been dead for over a year. Imagine the emotional complexity of living inside that situation: Would there not be an overwhelming desire to return to the amazing life you once had? Would a return to this life not seem *owed* to you?

When considered objectively, Simpson's public profile during the late 1990s accurately reflects the reasonable response of a stubborn, egocentric person who did not murder two people. In a weird way, it's the strongest argument in his favor (and maybe the only one). But it was a terrible, terrible move—and not just because I believe he murdered those two people. It would have been a terrible move even if he had not. He forced people to hate him, even if they barely cared.

* * *

It took me a while to figure out that Kareem Abdul-Jabbar was not beloved. When I became obsessed with basketball in 1980, he was my second-favorite player, and I just assumed this opinion was roughly shared by everyone (because Kareem was the *best* player, and—since I was eight—I assumed people were obligated to respect whoever was the best at anything). But I slowly got the impression my dad didn't like him, and neither did my older brothers. And whenever people interviewed him on TV (about anything that wasn't directly tied to a game he'd just finished), the questions always seemed obtuse and insulting, and Kareem always seemed annoyed or bored (or both). In January of that year, *Sports Illustrated* ran a profile on Abdul-Jabbar titled "A Different Drummer" that depicted itself as evidence that Abdul-Jabbar was becoming a more open, less moody superstar (*moody* was the word everybody always used). But this, of course, is not how magazine profiles operate. When a reporter claims that his or her subject is evolving in a positive manner, it's inevitably a way to catalog every unspecific criticism that has ever been levied against that subject in the past. It allows the reporter to be negative without taking any responsibility (because how can a story be considered a hit piece if the alleged takeaway is how the target is becoming a better person?). The story opens with a description of how a crowd at the Forum did not boo when informed by the PA announcer that Abdul-Jabbar had a migraine headache. Was Kareem supposed to feel good about this? Is he supposed to be elated that people didn't blame him for being incapacitated? Later, the writer asks Abdul-Jabbar how he felt about the way the media had reversed its position on him, suddenly deciding that he was a better player than Bill Walton (who they'd collectively argued was the more complete NBA center in 1977): "I view that with total cynicism," he replied. Which was both a) the correct answer and b) proof that he wasn't changing at all.

If you tried to sum up Abdul-Jabbar's lifelong problem with

the public into one thought, it would be that he was "not lik-able"—not necessarily *un*likable, but distant and difficult to love. He had an adversarial emotional compass; it seemed like you were supposed to appreciate him more than you were supposed to root for him, which is acceptable in every idiom except sport. Like so many unusually tall people, it was hard for Kareem to seem ecstatic about playing basketball. The profession didn't feel like his choice. For agile seven-foot skeletons, basketball is rarely an obsession. It's a game they are *pressured* to pursue, usually before they turn thirteen years old. [Former NBA guard Steve Kerr has noted that a key exception to this inclination is Tim Duncan, a six-foot-eleven adult whose infectious love for basketball mirrors that of a caffeinated five-foot-eleven schoolboy. This might explain why Duncan is liked by almost everyone, despite sharing the same stoic, mechanical demeanor as Abdul-Jabbar.] If a great tailback decides that football is barbaric, he can run track or wrestle; if a gifted shortstop finds baseball unsatisfying, he can usually excel at golf or tennis. Undersized hoop prodigies are inevitably good at every possible athletic pursuit, so they've consciously selected basketball over everything else. [I have no doubt that—had he chosen differently—Steve Nash would have been the greatest soc-cer player in Canadian history.] But such alternatives do not exist for human giants, and Kareem is the best example. This is not to say that he hated the game of basketball, because that would be untrue (if you count high school, he played it for twenty-eight consecutive years). All it means is that Abdul-Jabbar didn't really have agency in the matter. There was no better option for how he could spend his life. And what made Kareem so different was his total unwillingness to pretend that he did not know this.

There's a B-side from the rock band Pearl Jam titled "Sweet Lew," written by guitarist Jeff Ament (the "Lew" in its title refers to Jabbar's Christian name). If you listen to the song casually, you wouldn't immediately perceive it as a criticism of Abdul-Jabbar, as the lyrics are mostly complimentary and kind of juvenile ["*Wilt the Stilt had nothing on you / Lambchops and Afro-do, Milwaukee Bucks and a barbecue"*]. But Ament's interior motive for writing the song was based on a negative encounter he had with Abdul-Jabbar upon meeting him at a charity event. Ament (a lifelong hoop fan and a decent player as a high school student in Montana) was deeply hurt by Abdul-Jabbar's abject lack of interest toward his personal fandom. He didn't even pretend to care. This is telling. What made Pearl Jam dissimilar from their platinum-selling peers (most notably Nirvana) was that—despite being completely suffocated by a level of fame they did not anticipate—they still felt an obligation to appreciate the people who bought their records. Perhaps they did this naturally, or perhaps they did this as a social compulsion. Either way, Pearl Jam has always felt a responsibility to return whatever adoration was directed toward their existence. The motive of that return is beside the point, because the effort is what matters. It's certainly possible to dislike Pearl Jam's music, but you can't hate them as people, unless a) you believe they are somehow fake and b) you have some kind of teenage punk fixation on realness. To any normal person, a facsimile of gratitude is enough; that facsimile is an acceptable amount of emotional access. When Ament met Abdul-Jabbar, all Kareem needed to say was, "Thanks, man. That means a lot. Good luck with your life." He would not have needed to mean any of those words. Even if he'd been transparently acting, it would have been enough to satisfy a person who had pre-decided to love him. But Abdul-Jabbar can't do that. He can't ignore the stupidity of that false relationship, which is why a song like "Sweet Lew" exists. Kareem (being Kareem) loves jazz music—but even if he loved rock, he'd never relate to Pearl Jam (except for maybe "Corduroy"). He would prefer mid-period Rush: *"I can't pretend a stranger is a long-awaited friend."*

As he's moved into the winter of his life, Abdul-Jabbar has grown conscious of his image and has tried to evolve into a conventionally nice celebrity—which is disappointing on two levels. He has grown more patient with interviewers, partially because they have migrated to his side: It seems increasingly absurd that this intelligent, well-spoken, socially conscious person *who is the all-time leading scorer in the history of basketball* cannot get a job as an NBA head coach, simply because he's not super friendly. He had a cancer scare in 2008, so that generated some warranted sympathy; as an author, he's probably done more for the lost history of twentieth-century African-Americans than every other athlete combined. He made a cameo on a sitcom starring Zooey Deschanel, and it's so goofy and superfluous that only a jerk could criticize the decision. Muslims don't drink alcohol, but Kareem still endorsed Coors. If he's a villain, he's the best possible kind. Still, there are parts of his personal history that will never evaporate. He may ultimately be remembered more affectionately than anyone would have guessed in 1980, but that turnaround will always be framed as a surprise. He played the game, but he didn't play The Game. He refused to pretend that his life didn't feel normal to the person inside it, and he refused to pretend that other people's obsession with abnormality required him to act like the man he wasn't.

There's very little about the life of O. J. Simpson that could be classified as "under-reported." However, I can think of one element that totally is: His 2007 memoir, *If I Did It*. The existence of this book is deeply, vastly, hysterically underrated. My natural inclination is to try and compare it to something equally unusual, but I can't isolate a comparison. I want to write something along the lines of *"If I Did It* is as bizarre as _____," but no cultural minutia fits in that space. Roman Polanski would have to make a biopic about Charles Manson's music career.

Let me first describe what this book is: It's the nonfiction story of Simpson's relationship with Nicole Brown, plus one fictional chapter (near the end) in which O.J. explains how he would have killed Nicole, always staying within the facts and parameters of the actual homicide. After 123 pages of straightforward romantic

memoir, O.J. casually drops in the following one-sentence paragraph . . .

Now picture this—and keep in mind, this is hypothetical:

What follows that sentence are fifteen pages written exactly like
the previous 123, except that we are now supposed to assume
all the actions described are some nightmarish fantasy Simpson
created for our entertainment. When I first purchased the book,
I assumed this section would be a description of "murder strategy," in which O.J. describes how a clever person would have
committed these crimes (as opposed to the brutal, unsubtle manner in which they actually occurred). But this is not the case.
Instead O.J. creates a second character (a fellow he calls Charlie) who rides along with him to Brown's bungalow and watches
him stab Brown and Goldman to death in an act of animalistic
rage. Nothing is delivered in a theoretical context. There's lots
of profane dialogue throughout the passage, and the phrases are
amazingly specific (at one point, O.J. imagines himself saying,
"Fuck that. I'm tired of being the understanding ex-husband").
When he "fictionalizes" the physical confrontation with Goldman, he describes his adversary's fighting posture precisely and
mocks Goldman's attempts at karate. It's expressed like a memory, and I'm almost certain that's what it is. The inclusion of the
Charlie character is the only thing that makes it seem unlike the
conventional view of what happened that night; I'm not sure if
Charlie is supposed to be a literary device (so that O.J. has a vessel
to turn his interior monologue into a printable conversation) or
if this is some perverse attempt at implicating Simpson's buddy
A. C. Cowlings as an accessory to murder. The "fabricated" anec-
dote ends back at Simpson's residence, where O.J. describes how
he would (did?) manage to sneak back into the house and take
a shower before leaving for LAX and flying to Chicago; at this
point, *If I Did It* resumes being a memoir, in which Simpson

gives his account of the arrest and the days that followed (it also includes a full transcript of his first interview with the LAPD). In other words, this is a short book in which a guy intimately describes his bad marriage (which is supposed to be real), how that relationship made him feel (which is also supposed to be real), a detailed account of his ex-wife's murder (which is supposed to be *unreal*), and the man's memories of what happened in the wake of her death (which is not only real, but verified by audio tape). And it's all written in the same voice, seemingly for the same purpose.

The story behind the publication of *If I Did It* is part of the reason this book is destined to become a lost artifact, despite its temporary status as a bestseller: The book was originally a pure money grab: Simpson and his cowriter (screenwriter Pablo Fenjves, a neighbor of Brown's who paradoxically testified *against* O.J. during the '94 trial) were to cobble the book together for Judith Regan, a highly successful, highly unscrupulous publishing magnate with HarperCollins, a company owned by News Corp. The machinations of what was really going on here remain unclear; Fenjves was told that the revenue would go toward Simpson's children, while Regan later alleged that her only motive for publishing the memoir was to prove Simpson's guilt. Regardless, the book was aborted before it came out. The public was predictably outraged by what it assumed *If I Did It* would be, and further incensed by a TV special that was intended to coincide with the book's release (in theory, Barbara Walters was going to interview Simpson during the November ratings sweeps). For a moment, it looked as if *If I Did It* would never exist. (HarperCollins reportedly destroyed four hundred thousand copies of the book before it went on sale.) But then something even more bizarre occurred: A bankruptcy court in Florida awarded the rights to *If I Did It* to Ron Goldman's estate. As one might expect, the Goldman family had always been very, very against the book on the grounds that it exploited the death of their son. But Simpson (despite his victory in the criminal trial) had been found guilty in the civil suit filed by the Goldmans and now owed them $33 million. And since Simpson was living in Florida—a state whose bankruptcy laws were heavily tilted in O.J.'s favor—the Goldmans were never going to see any of that money. So a judge decreed that the Goldmans could publish *If I Did It* as financial compensation for Ron Goldman's death. The family made some key changes to the book's presentation, most notably the addition of a not-so-subtle subtitle ("Confessions of the Killer") and one of the most consciously misleading book covers in the history of literature: The words I DID IT are printed as large as possible in red, while the minuscule word IF is lodged inside the letter *I*.

My copy doesn't even have O.J.'s name on the cover, a crazy idea that makes total sense. The reason it makes sense is that people still do not like the idea of O. J. Simpson writing this book. They want to imagine that the book was created against his will. If you don't believe me, try reading *If I Did It* in public. The moment anyone figures out what you're actually holding, they reflexively embrace (or feign) disgust.

"Why would you want to read that?" a writer friend of mine asked when I told him how fascinating it was.

"Because it's a murderer writing about murdering people while still pretending he's innocent," I said. "It's totally unique. Would you prefer to read an essay by a journalist who interviewed O.J. about this situation?"

"Well, yes," said my friend. "That would be great."

"Would you want to read a roman à clef about an ex–football player who murders two people and escapes prosecution?"

"That might also be okay," said my friend. "It would depend on the execution. But those are different situations. It's just fucked up that O.J. is the author of the book you're reading."

"He didn't make any money off it," I replied. "Why is someone interpreting the event a better source than the person directly involved?"

"Because he's obviously lying," my friend said. "And it's just weird."

It *is* weird. That's true. The book is nuts. But that really wasn't my friend's argument. He was using the word *weird* in place of the word *wrong,* because *wrong* seems self-righteous. "It's just wrong" seems like something Mitch Albom would say about *If I Did It.* But this wrongness—this abstract wrongness that can't be verbally justified, because it harms no one—is why O. J. Simpson is despised in such a culturally penetrating context. It's a hatred that transcends his alleged crimes or his ability to divert justice. When Lizzie Borden was acquitted of her parents' murder in 1893, the people of New England were outraged—but Lizzie didn't *taunt the public* for failing to convict her. She just moved into a nice house with her sister and became a recluse. A century later, Borden is "hated" by no one; anyone captivated by her life is predisposed to think about the murders from her perspective (and to hunt for any clue that might validate her improbable innocence). Over time, the public will grow to accept almost any terrible act committed by a celebrity; everything eventually becomes interesting to those who aren't personally involved. But Simpson does not allow for uninvolvement. He exceeds the acceptable level of self-directed notoriety and changes the polarity of the event; by writing this book, he makes it seem like the worst part of Brown and Goldman's murder was what happened *to him,* and that he perversely wants the world to *remember* that he killed them (even if he's somehow internally convinced himself that he did not, which is what I always assumed during the trial). He keeps reminding people that he is famous because two other people are dead.

There are many, many sports fans who believe Kobe Bryant raped a woman in 2003 and was never penalized. Nothing— *nothing*—has happened in the subsequent ten years that would lead anyone to be convinced Kobe was wrongly accused. But Bryant refuses to acknowledge that the incident even occurred. He won't answer any question related to the accusation and just pretends like he doesn't remember anything about it. A lot of people still hate him for this, but they can't access the incident in question. It's now a footnote to the rest of his life. They have to hate him for other things, so they accuse him of shooting too much and being a terrible teammate and trying to be cooler than he actually is. We have to inject our distaste for his alleged crime into things that don't really matter, so most of the criticism comes across as unfair and ad hominem. Kobe (probably) did something bad in Colorado, but he handled it perfectly. O.J. keeps doing the opposite. He elects to tell a terrible story that cannot *not* be interesting, because he's the only person alive who can know what he knows. There is no comparable text to *If I Did It*. If the only thing that mattered about reality was the proliferation of information and perspective, it would be an invaluable document. But nobody thinks this way, except maybe me. *If I Did It* teaches us nothing we consciously want to know. It only proves that O.J. knows the most about what happened on June 12, and that he doesn't care at all.

In *Airplane!*, Kareem Abdul-Jabbar portrays Roger Murdock, the doomed aircraft's copilot. However, the principal comedic utility is that he's really playing himself (but refuses to admit it). His most memorable scene is when a little kid enters the cockpit, instantly recognizes him, and says, "I think you're the greatest, but my dad thinks you don't work hard enough on defense." It's funny, but also smart: Movie Kareem pretends to be offended by the remark, but Real Kareem clearly finds the criticism amusing (or else he wouldn't have allowed it in the script). It shows a sense of humor that he had never presented before. But the joke is bigger than that. The core of the joke is that it's ridiculous to pretend that Kareem Abdul-Jabbar is anyone besides himself. You can't be a seven-foot-two character actor; even if Kareem had the acting chops of Philip Seymour Hoffman, he can't disappear into another being. He can only be who he is, and even a child can see this. So the center of the joke (better known as the unfunny part of the joke) is that Kareem is denying who he obviously is. He wants to disappear into society, and that's impossible. It's something everyone can understand in theory, but nobody accepts in practice. He is supposed to be happier than he is. He is supposed to *like* being Kareem Abdul-Jabbar, and he's supposed to like that we like it, too.

Before 9/11 happened, we used to think O.J.'s Bronco chase was going to be the last collectively shared moment in America. "The culture is splintering," people like me would postulate, "and this wacky circumstance will mark the last night everyone watched the same thing at the same time." I probably wrote those exact words at some point in 1994, which is ridiculous for multiple reasons—but the main reason it's ridiculous is because I never saw one second of that police chase.

I missed the whole thing.

Now, I realize I'm not the only adult in America who didn't watch this event while it transpired. But I'm the only adult I know who missed it in totality. I was at a movie. I had just moved to Fargo a few days before, and my cable still wasn't hooked up. My apartment was just boxes stacked upon boxes. I had to choose between watching game five of the NBA Finals in a bar or seeing the movie *Backbeat* downtown. Either way, I was going to be alone. I decided to watch the fake Beatles in a big dark room. The film was disappointing. For some reason, I sat through all the credits, which I normally never do (I guess I was being "extra alone"). I finally walked to my car, parked diagonally on a popular street that was completely empty. Seconds after I turned the ignition key, the radio DJ artlessly interrupted the intro of a song (I believe it was "Runaway Train") and said something baffling: "We've just received word that O. J. Simpson's white Ford Bronco is parked in front of his house. O. J. Simpson has parked his Bronco in front of his house." I remember being mad about this. I remember thinking, "The media is out of control. How is this news?" I drove home, still thinking about my disappointment with the movie. I entered my dark apartment and saw the light on my answering machine blinking way too rapidly. I pressed the button and was mechanically informed that I had fourteen messages. I rarely got fourteen messages in any given month. This is bad, I thought to myself. Someone has died.

But the messages were all from different people, and none of them made sense.

"Chuck! Are you watching this? Call me if you're watching this." (*beep*)

"This . . . this is the craziest fucking thing . . . this is the craziest fucking thing I've ever seen." (*beep*)

"Why is he doing this? Is this real?" (*beep*)

One of the last messages happened to mention O.J. by name, so I deduced that this really *was* about death (although not anybody who hadn't already been dead yesterday). I turned on the television; even without cable, I could get a fuzzy version of Fox. I started calling people back, and they told me what I'd missed. It was an easy story to explain, because nothing actually happened. A man nobody had ever heard of drove a sports utility vehicle while his famous passenger pointed a gun at his head and was cheered by idiots. It was a little like the end of *The Blues Brothers,* but way slower.

Because I missed this event, I think about it a lot. I don't know why. [I'm tempted to make up some capricious, impossible explanation that would make sense within this essay, but I'll resist.] Earlier that day, while I was sitting at my desk at the newspaper that employed me, the TV next to the copy desk had aired footage of Simpson's friend and lawyer Richard Kardashian reading a four-page letter from O.J.: At the time, no one was able to locate Simpson, and the letter seemed like a rather unambiguous suicide note (everything about O.J.'s life was written in the past tense). I recall a few reporters speculating that O.J. might kill himself, but the speculation was casual. For the most part, working-class people were not yet obsessed with this state of affairs—the inception of that worldwide phenomenon was still eight hours away. For one final afternoon, O.J. News still seemed like News of the Weird. But I've often wondered what would have happened if O.J. really had shot himself that day (which might have been his original intention). Suicide would have galvanized his guilt irrefutably, and it would have erased him from the earth. But people would definitely like him more than they do now.

As I write this, O. J. Simpson sits in the Lovelock Correction Center, a medium-security prison in northwest Nevada. It's uncomfortable to make the following statement, but it must be made: O.J. is serving an unjust sentence. In 2007, he tried to steal back a collection of his own memorabilia from a hotel room in Las Vegas, and he used a gun. That was stupid. However, he was somehow convicted of kidnapping for doing so, which is equally idiotic. He could face up to thirty-three years in prison for this crime (although a Nevada judge reopened the case in the fall of 2012). Everyone concedes that his sentence was backdoor retribution for the murders he was acquitted of; no one in power can directly admit this, but nobody can deny it without seeming naïve. I feel no sympathy for Simpson. But I wonder: Does O.J. realize that this (technically unjust) sentence was his best-case scenario? Does he comprehend how his forced disappearance from society is perhaps the only thing that will salvage whatever remains of his legacy? Is he aware how much people hated his unwillingness to behave like someone he wasn't?

He will never, ever be free. At least now he doesn't have to try.

HITLER IS IN THE BOOK

So here was my problem: I was not going to write about Adolf Hitler.

It did not seem like a prudent move. What was the upside? I certainly did not want to write anything that could be misinterpreted as an apology for Hitler, which seemed (almost inescapably) likely, unless I just typed the sentence "Hitler was evil" over and over and over, the same way Jack Nicholson typed "All work and no play makes Jack a dull boy" in *The Shining*. I also saw no benefit in writing about how Hitler was a bad person, since no one needs to read a book that informs them of what everyone already knows. I thought I could just write around his existence, or just sprinkle in a few references when writing about other people, or maybe write about him in a way that made it seem like he wasn't actually there. But whenever I mentioned this to people (and particularly when I mentioned it to Jewish acquaintances), they found this strategy troubling. "Hitler is in the book," one of these acquaintances said during a casual Chinese dinner. No, I responded. You must have misheard me. I said Hitler is not going to be in the book. "Then you're doing it wrong," he said. *"Hitler is in the book."*

So I decided this guy had a point.

I decided that Hitler would be in the book. I would write an essay about Hitler. But as soon as I made this decision, everything changed. Everyone now told me the opposite of everything they'd told me before.

"You better make sure you let your agent read whatever you write before you try to publish it," said my closest friend. My friend is Jewish (and so is my agent). "People will go crazy if you write about Hitler. It doesn't matter what your argument is. You can't write about Hitler. It's just one of those things." When he said *you can't write about Hitler,* I could not tell if he was talking about non-Jews in general or me in specific. [I now suspect he might have meant "non-serious non-Jews," a literary category I dominate.]

Because I worry about everything, I started worrying about this. I started wondering how this could possibly be done, assuming every person who advised me on this issue was simultaneously correct.

There seemed to be two central contradictions at play.

The first was that it would only make sense to write about Hitler if I had something new to say about him—something that no one else had expressed before (since such an attempt could only be justified if there was more at stake than facile entertainment or narrative obligation). The second was that I could not contradict the preexisting vision of Hitler within the public consciousness; whatever I wrote would need to reflect the prevailing view of who he was and what he believed (because there are certain aspects of society that are not open for debate). The Hitler I described had to be the Hitler we collectively imagine and accept.

So here is the new problem: I have no choice but to write about Adolf Hitler, despite the fact that writing about Hitler is a terrible idea. And I have to write something creative about him, but without writing anything that isn't already established and accepted. I have to do something I shouldn't do, and I have to be interesting without being interesting.

At least it will be short.

Since his suicide in 1945, there's been a worldwide obsession with "explaining" Hitler. This is most easily seen in Ron Rosenbaum's aptly titled book, *Explaining Hitler*. Published in 1998, it's great for multiple reasons, many of which only serve to increase my fear over writing anything about Hitler that anyone could care about in any way whatsoever. In the book's introduction, we learn that Claude Lanzmann, the French filmmaker who directed the nine-and-a-half-hour Holocaust documentary *Shoah,* was outraged over the very notion of using Hitler's baby photo as the *Explaining Hitler* cover image (in essence, Lanzmann was offended by any visual image that forces people to consider Hitler as an innocent person). The final quarter of the book tackles the various theories on what caused Hitler to enforce the genocide that defined him, primarily examined through the perspective of various writers and academics. The opinions run the gamut of human possibility: There's an argument that blames the social history of Germany, an argument that suggests anti-Semitism is intrinsic to Christian culture, a contention that Hitler was somehow akin to Shakespeare's Hamlet, and a claim that Hitler had already decided to exterminate the Jewish race as early as November of 1918 (and that *everything* that happened in World War II was solely the product of this one singular obsession, and that all historical evidence to the contrary is simply Hitler being esoteric and duplicitous on purpose). Some of these theories are stronger than others; none is entirely devoid of merit. Still, one passage near the end of *Explaining Hitler* struck me as the most meaningful, perhaps because it instantly illustrates why every attempt at explaining Hitler collides with the same philosophical wall. What follows is Rosenbaum writing about Emil Fackenheim, a Jewish rabbi and philosopher who died in 2003:

> Fackenheim . . . makes an exceptionalist argument about Hitler and human nature: You cannot locate Hitler on the ordinary continuum of human nature; you cannot merely say that he is a very, very, very, very, very bad man, perhaps the most wicked yet, but still explicable as the product of the same human

nature, the same psychological forces that produced, say, the next-worst human being and the next and the next until we reach ourselves. No, Fackenheim says, Hitler is off the charts, off the grid, in another category of radical evil entirely.

I do not bring this up to dispute or support Fackenheim's claim, but to acknowledge how casually entrenched this belief has become within every context of Hitler's role in popular culture. It is, really, the only way to talk about Hitler in a casual manner. You can't compare other people to Hitler without immediately seeming unhinged and unreasonable (whenever this happens—be it in the real world of politics or in the comments section of a website—the debate immediately becomes unserious). If you're going to make jokes about him, you need to go full-on absurd: "As I told the tribunal at Nuremberg, I did not know Hitler was a Nazi," Woody Allen writes in his short story "The Schmeed Memoirs." "I thought he worked for the phone company." Hitler is still a historical figure, but he's predominantly a placeholder for cognitive darkness; he's the entity we use in the same way people once employed the devil. But the devil is no longer a villain in pop culture. The devil is sympathetic. He's charming. If you're making a movie about the devil, you cast Al Pacino. In the pop world, the devil is mostly depicted as a fair-minded gambler; if you're a good enough musician, the devil will give you a golden fiddle and concede his defeat, allowing you to peacefully live the rest of your days in rural Georgia. There really isn't "another category of radical evil." That category has a population of one.

There's a song from 1963 that inadvertently proves this.

The song is titled "With God on Our Side," written and performed by Bob Dylan (the fact that Dylan is the singer is extremely important, since he's just about the only unassailable figure in pop culture). The song is primarily a criticism of how history is dictated by whoever ends up winning and the problematic certitude of Judeo-Christians who believe God always supports whatever it is they happen to be doing. There are, I suppose, two ways to interpret the lyrics of this song. One would be to take them literally (also known as "the wrong way to interpret this song"). The other would be to view them as ironic (which suggests that Dylan believes God is on no one's side, and that there is really no side for God to take). It's the difference between thinking the song praises God and thinking the song isn't about God at all.

There are two verses that particularly matter to me, at least as they apply to Hitler. One of these is the fifth verse, which goes like this:

> When the Second World War
> Came to an end
> We forgave the Germans
> And we were friends
> Though they murdered six million
> In the ovens they fried
> The Germans now too
> Have God on their side

It seems obvious that Dylan is expressing bewilderment over the fact that the country we hoped to destroy during the war had become a key American ally less than twenty years later. He's referring to people like Wernher von Braun, the physicist who developed the V-2 rocket for the Nazis in 1937 before taking a job with the U.S. military in 1945. Dylan's ethnic Judaism probably contributed to this sentiment. There's really only one way to read and understand the words of this verse; they are not ambiguous. When talking about the world of Hitler, even Dylan—the most unreliable narrator in rock history—strives for clarity. But compare those words with the language he uses in the eighth verse, which is the most memorable passage from the song:

Through many a dark hour
I've been thinkin' about this
That Jesus Christ
Was betrayed by a kiss
But I can't think for you
You'll have to decide
Whether Judas Iscariot
Had God on his side

This section is far more complicated (and consciously so). It might be an edgy attempt to make people consider the absurdity of assuming God is on their side simply because they want that to be true (and Dylan uses Judas as the ultimate example of God's misappropriation). It's equally possible that the message is literal but paradoxical: If Dylan is working from the perspective that Christianity is a positive thing, then Jesus Christ *had* to be crucified in order to rise from the dead (which would mean Judas truly did have God's support, simply because there was no other way). The fact that Dylan is telling listeners that they must decide this question for themselves might suggest that he feels this problem is unknowable; the fact that he mentions Judas Iscariot (the most overtly negative stereotype of Judaism within the New Testament) might imply a theological critique. Regardless, the eighth verse of "With God on Our Side" allows for something the fifth verse does not: acceptable misinterpretation. It's totally okay to hear those lines and get the wrong idea (in some ways, being wrong actually makes the work more interesting). You can inflexibly believe Dylan is somehow relating to (or sympathizing with) Judas, and the song is still a classic. But there is no way Dylan could have allowed for the possibility of any misinterpretation in the aforementioned fifth verse. Imagine, just for a moment, that the fifth verse read, "We forgave Hitler" (or if the eighth verse implied that—in his darkest hour—Dylan found himself wondering if even Hitler had God on his side). It would not matter if his larger artistic intent was exactly the same; if any percentage of his audience erroneously believed that Dylan was authentically confused about how he should feel about Hitler, his career is changed forever. Some would compare him to David Allan Coe, and "With God on Our Side" would eventually be covered by Skrewdriver. Even in a country that is 80 percent Christian—and even though Christians traditionally view Judas Iscariot as the most deceitful soldier in Satan's eternal army—Judas is not Hitler. He's not even close. He seems maybe one third as bad, even if the Gospels' description of his life is taken to be 100 percent accurate.

Nobody ever talks about building a time machine in order to go back and kill Judas.

I have a friend with numerous historical obsessions, one of which is twentieth-century dictators. Sometimes we get boozed up and chat about "the Big Three": Hitler, Joseph Stalin, and Mao Tsetung—the Beatles, Stones, and Zeppelin of despotic human misery. The average American doesn't tend to know much about Stalin outside of his Ruthian statistics: He killed between twenty and fifty million people during his time as leader of the Soviet Union, which (in the saddest possible way) makes him "underrated." It's believed Stalin caused the death of five million people in the Ukraine alone from imposed starvation. It's possible Mao killed even more humans than Stalin (journalist Jonathan Fenby once suggested the total might be around seventy million), but his reputation is somehow obscured (if not necessarily improved) by all the bizarre eccentricities we know about his personal life: A book written by Mao's longtime physician Li Zhisui, *The Private Life of Chairman Mao*, exhaustively chronicles the leader's unwillingness to brush his teeth, his maniacal fixations on sex and swimming, and his desire for luxuries that were alien to his starving countrymen (during a 1958 tour of a desperately poor Chinese province, Mao's motorcade was followed by a watermelon truck). Every so often, someone will make the argument that Stalin and

Mao were just as bad as Hitler, and that the reason certain tyrants are hated more than others illustrates a larger problem with how history is understood, particularly by white people. It's not a terrible argument, but it doesn't change reality—as an anecdotal culture, we know more about Hitler than we do about every other despot combined. It's possible that the information we have about Stalin and Mao is less than the amount of *disinformation* we have about Hitler. For example, many people seem to believe that Hitler had only one testicle (and that this monorchism explains his diabolical nature). Some historians have spent years investigating this belief, and most conclude that it's an urban legend. But this is further evidence of Hitler's exceptionalism: I can't think of any other public figure whose scrotum feels historically meaningful (or disputed).

Just start with his appearance: At what age could you have drawn a recognizable sketch of Adolf Hitler? I could have done so when I was six. But what percentage of North Americans could even identify a photo of Stalin (much less sketch a version of their own)? The vision of Hitler is so engrained in people's minds that NBA legend Michael Jordan was roundly ridiculed for appearing in an underwear commercial with a mustache that *vaguely resembled* the one worn by Hitler. Have you ever wanted to upset people at a dinner party? Mention the fact that Hitler was a vegetarian. A handful of guests will immediately lose their minds. They will go on to cite the numerous revisionists who now claim that Hitler was not a true vegetarian and that his dietician secretly added bone marrow to his vegetable soup. [It has never really been clear—to me, or to anyone else—what the debate over Hitler's diet was supposed to prove. I honestly think it began as an absurdist way to tease vegetarians, a group not known for their winning sense of humor. However, all the impassioned denials from the vegetarian community make me wonder if people took this joke as a serious attack on their lifestyle. When someone tries to argue that Hitler occasionally ate meat, is the subtext that no true vegetarian could possibly commit genocide? Is there some unspoken fear inside vegetarians that prompts them to worry that what they are doing is somehow wrong, despite the fact that it (assumedly) feels morally correct? Does it mean that Hitler was so evil that it's wrong to *eat* like him?] We know quite a bit about Hitler's alleged love life. In fact, we know so much about it that the data is useless: It ranges from the possibility that Hitler was asexual to the idea that he was involved with seven "suicide maidens," six of whom successfully or unsuccessfully committed suicide as a result of Hitler's ultra-depraved sexual desires (the lone non-suicidal maiden is alleged to be the Nazi filmmaker Leni Riefenstahl, whose relationship with the führer is usually described as intense but platonic . . . and, judging from her films, extremely long and slightly boring).

A lot of what we "know" about Hitler seems unimportant. It often seems closer to gossip than history. But Hitler's social role requires gossip; unlike Mao or Stalin, he needs to seem extra-alive and uniquely human. This is because we do not hate Hitler as an abstraction; we hate him *as Hitler*. It's not enough to be against his principles or the specter of Nazism. Hitler is hated as a specific person, if only to remind us that the Holocaust occurred because of a specific person's work. Now, I realize the same argument could be made for almost every man-made tragedy throughout time; in every case, some specific individual was ultimately writing the checks. But Hitler allows us not to worry about all those other dictators in any specialized sense. Hitler is the human catch-all for all other terrible humans. Other genocides can be viewed as sinister in concept and heartbreaking in practice, but without any pressure to understand and personify the men who made them happen. Mao and Stalin (and Hirohito and Amin and Leopold and Robespierre) are dead, both literally *and* figuratively. They are historic caricatures. They can disappear. But we need to keep Hitler alive. Hitler needs to be a person we hate on a one-to-one basis. He's the worst. That's his job.

* * *

During the druggiest periods of his life, David Bowie loved talking about Hitler. "Rock stars are fascists," he told *Playboy* in 1976. "Adolf Hitler was one of the first rock stars." This is not a compliment, but rather a criticism—in typical Bowie fashion, he consciously made a statement he knew would be misconstrued by anyone who didn't read the entire interview. In 1971, he wrote a song called "Quicksand" that certainly *seems* to be about Hitler, sung from the deranged perspective of Hitler's inner monologue during the final moments of his life. The chorus features some of Bowie's most unsettling lyric writing, sung with a fragility that's both spectral and matter-of-fact:

> Don't believe in yourself
> Don't deceive with belief
> Knowledge comes
> With death's release

What this means is debatable; I think Bowie is simultaneously painting these sentiments as pathetic (when applied to Hitler) and uncomfortably true (when pushed through the worldview of the songwriter). They become even more accidentally insightful in light of the discovery of the diary of Guy Liddell, the deputy of Nazi counterespionage. Liddell's 1945 journal recounts one of Hitler's final rants, when the dictator allegedly claimed, "Everyone has lied to me, everyone has deceived me, no one has told me the truth. The armed forces have lied to me and now the SS have left me in the lurch. The German people has not fought heroically, it deserves to perish. It is not I who have lost the war, but the German people." He then experienced a nervous breakdown, setting the table for Bowie's speculative fiction. It's a complicated, not wholly implausible scenario. But this much is clear: Even an artist like Bowie—a subversive contrarian obsessed with Berlin—could not fully don the mask of Hitler. The closest he comes is imagining the dictator's remorseful dying thoughts, when even Adolf realizes he was wrong about everything.

There is, I suppose, another reason I was hesitant to write about Hitler (and this has nothing to do with any fear of reprisals): Hitler contradicts the thesis I've been promoting for 193 pages. I keep hammering this point about how villains are inevitably the people who know the most and care the least. But Adolf Hitler is the opposite. Hitler cared very, very much about many perverse things. He cared about the supremacy of Germany. He cared about exterminating the Jews. He cared about Luz Long's long-jump performance at the 1936 Olympics. He cared like crazy. But I don't think he knew the most, or even very much, about things that mattered. This applies to big questions ("Is it wrong to kill off an entire race of people in order to solve unclear problems?") but also to practical matters ("Should we fight a land war in Russia during winter?"). I'm not suggesting he was an imbecile; it just seems like his success was mostly a product of his prowess as a public speaker. [Whenever sane historians try to paint an objective portrait of Hitler, the only two non-negative words they feel comfortable expressing are *efficient* (which immediately becomes darkly pejorative within the context of the Holocaust) and *charismatic*. Hitler remains the best argument against charisma.]

Hitler cared so much, in fact, that his imagined emotion is now hilarious. Probably the single funniest Internet meme of the early twenty-first century were numerous parodies of the climactic scene from the 2004 film *Der Untergang,* a cinematic depiction of the last days of the Third Reich (the film's title translates as *Downfall* and was based on Joachim Fest's book *Inside Hitler's Bunker*). I assume anyone reading this book will have seen at least one of these clips: Amateur editors take the scene—spoken entirely in German—and change the subtitles so that Hitler is losing his mind over the cancellation of *Ugly Betty* or the ineptitude of the 2008 Detroit Lions. I'm not sure why this is so funny, but I think

it has something to do with the fabricated idea of Hitler's personality—it's funny to think of Hitler as this emotional, uniformed
lunatic who is (above all) superficial. It's not just that an apoplectic
Hitler is frothing at the mouth and screaming at his underlings;
it's that he's frothing and screaming about the film adaptation
of *Twilight* or his inability to get an iPhone. These memes aren't
criticisms of Hitler, because they're too ridiculous—however, we
don't need Hitler to be criticized in any new way (because he's
already the universal placeholder for evil). What we need are new
ways to make Hitler seem *present*. He just needs to be there. The
rest we can do on our own.

THE PROBLEM OF
OVERRATED IDEAS

Writing about other people is a form of writing about oneself. This isn't true for everyone, but it's true for me. Why pretend?

In 2004, I wrote a column for *Esquire* that was headlined, "The Importance of Being Hated." It was the kind of piece that was (sort of) funny and (sort of) true, and the combination of those two qualities somehow metabolized and made the funny parts funnier and the true parts super true. The crux of the essay dealt with the difference between a "nemesis" and an "archenemy." Not many people remember this column, but—if they do, and if they want to talk to me about it—they inevitably remember the last half of one specific paragraph:

I've had the same archenemy since eighth grade: He's a guy named Rick Helling, and he grew up in Lakota, North Dakota. Last year, Helling pitched a few innings for the Florida Marlins in the World Series; in 1998, he won twenty games for the Texas Rangers. I went to basketball camp with Rick Helling in 1985, and he was the single worst person I'd ever met. Every summer, I constantly scan the sports section of *USA Today*, always hoping that he got shelled. This is what drives me. I cannot live in a world where Helling's career ERA hovers below 5.00, yet all I do for a living is type. As long as Rick Helling walks this earth, I shall never sleep soundly.

The reason this is (sort of) funny is because it's idiotic, and I'm (sort of) positioning myself in the role of idiot. It obviously makes no sense to hate someone I knew for only one week, twenty years ago. I never truly knew Rick Helling at all, and—even if I had—I knew him when he was an eighth grader. It's also more than coincidental that the person I elected to classify as my arch-enemy is the only major league baseball player I ever happened to encounter as an adolescent. But the reason it's (sort of) true is because *it's sort of true*. I have never gotten over what a sublime jerk Rick Helling was during that week at basketball camp. I still think about it today. He shot three-pointers constantly and never passed to anyone. He was physically stronger than every kid his age, yet aspired to be a point guard and refused to play under the basket (this drove me especially crazy, as I envied his size and power). He was obsessed with talking about sex (which I suppose made him a normal eighth grader, but which I found disturb-ing). He constantly complained about the officiating and totally ignored the advisement of our coach. Mainly, he was an egocen-tric bully: One afternoon, the camp directors created a two-on-two tournament, and they tried to make all the teams as equal as possible. They paired Rick with some microscopic rich kid who was probably only at camp because his parents wanted him out of the house; I remember that the kid always wore a massive wrist-watch (even during games) and looked like he'd spent the last six months recovering from cancer in rural Ethiopia. I doubt if he secured one rebound that entire week. But Helling was so god-damn good, it didn't matter—the kid with the wristwatch would just pass him the ball immediately and watch Helling play two-on-one. They made it all the way to the title game, only to lose by a basket . . . at which point Helling punted the ball into the rafters and started stomping toward his pip-squeak teammate like a griz-zly bear gorged on bath salts. Had the camp counselors not inter-vened, that child was destined for the morgue (although at least he'd have known the exact time of his death). When I think about

Rick Helling, these are the things I think about. It's the reason I ambushed him in *Esquire,* despite the fact that a) I didn't *really* care that any of this had happened, and b) I was pretty confident that Rick had no memory of who I was.

Now, something weird happened immediately after that column was published: While pitching in a spring training game against the Phillies, a line drive hit Helling in the leg and broke his fibula. I felt terrible about this, specifically because I'd written the sentence "As long as Rick Helling walks this earth, I shall never sleep soundly." I certainly didn't believe I had cosmically *caused* this injury, but I didn't like that I'd expressed a desire for a man to cease walking just before his leg shattered. It was not the type of irony I was looking for. My obsession with Helling had always been semi-performative, but now it seemed sick. I decided to just stop thinking about Rick Helling entirely; this was not difficult, particularly after his 2007 retirement. But then—in 2009—I happened to be reading an issue of *Time* magazine (I think I was waiting to see the dentist). The magazine was running an excerpt from *The Yankee Years,* Joe Torre's book written with Tom Verducci. The piece was headlined THE MAN WHO WARNED BASEBALL ABOUT STEROIDS.

To my horror, I realized the Man they were referring to was Rick Helling.

For all practical purposes, Helling will be remembered as the first player in Major League Baseball to take a meaningful stand against performance-enhancing drugs. The year was 1998: Baseball was spiking in popularity, mostly due to the explosion of home runs by Mark McGwire (who'd hit seventy that summer) and Sammy Sosa (who'd hit sixty-six). Though it seems insane in retrospect, no one wanted to admit that this uptick in power was unnatural . . . except, evidently, Rick Helling. At that winter's players union meeting, Helling, who was only twenty-seven, stood up and said, "There is this problem with steroids. It's happening. It's real. And it's so prevalent that guys who aren't doing it are feeling pressure because they're falling behind. It's not a level playing field. We've got to figure out a way to address it . . . It's one thing to be a cheater, to be somebody who doesn't care whether it's right or wrong. But it's another thing when other guys feel like they have to do it just to keep up." Nobody paid any attention to his ideas, so he delivered the same speech the following year. And he made it the year after that, and the year after that, and the year after that. And nobody cared, until they did. Helling had a nice career as a player (93 career wins, 1,058 strikeouts), but this was his real achievement. This is why he'll be (justifiably) remembered by baseball historians. They will remember him as a truth pioneer.

So here's my life: The one person I am on record for hating is the first baseball player on record for taking a public stand against anabolic steroids.

I have tried to rationalize my way out of this reality. I've reversed my position on steroids several times. I've tried to imagine that Helling's speech was grandstanding, or that it's the typical behavior of a narcissistic personality. But I can't unread that book excerpt. Here's Helling's final quote, spoken as a retired activist, lodged in the article's penultimate paragraph: "Anybody who knows me knows there was no doubt that I played it the right way. And that's what I wanted to leave the game with. I couldn't care less if I made one million dollars or one hundred million dollars, whether I won one game or whether I won three hundred games. I was in it to be honest to myself and to my teammates and to be a good father and husband. For me, it was just the way I was brought up."

Those words make me think many things. However, they mainly make me think one thing: *He's lying*. I don't believe what he says, even though he has no reason to fabricate any of it. I just can't see him as good. So I read those words again, and I read them again, and I read them again. I continue to absorb them as lies. I see them as small lies inside of larger lies. I try to make them what I want them to be. And—eventually—a feeling creeps over my shoulders and up my neck. It's a feeling I've felt my whole life, and it's a feeling I know I will have forever.

In my own story, I am the villain.

Rick Helling is not a bad guy because of what I remember from 1985; I am a bad guy *because I remember it* (and because it informs how I think about everything else). I know it's wrong and I do it anyway. I do it consciously. I have the ability to think about this person in a thousand different contexts, yet I prefer keeping my mind unchanged. I can see every alternate reality, but I prefer to arbitrarily create my own. I know the truth, but I just don't care.

It's natural to think of one's own life as a novel (or a movie or a play), and within that narrative we are always the central character. Thoughtful people try to overcome this compulsion, but they usually fail (in fact, trying makes it worse). In a commencement speech at Kenyon College, David Foster Wallace argued that conquering the preoccupation with self is pretty much the whole objective of being alive—but if we are to believe Wallace succeeded at this goal, it must be the darkest success imaginable. I'm far less confident than DFW. I don't think it's feasible (I think people can pretend to do it, but they can't pretend to themselves). I have slowly come to believe that overcoming this self-focused worldview is impossible, and that life can be experienced only through an imaginary mirror that allows us to occupy the center of a story no one is telling. I don't think the human mind is capable of getting outside of that box, and I'm not even sure if this limitation is particularly problematic. I never feel weird about being the main character in the nontransferable, nonexistent movie of my life. That's totally fine. What makes me nervous is a growing suspicion that this movie is fucked up and devoid of meaning. The auteur is a nihilist. What if I'm the main character, but still not the protagonist? *What if there is no protagonist?* What if there's just an uninteresting person, thinking about himself because there's nothing else to think about?

I wear the plaid hat.

ACKNOWLEDGMENTS

Chuck Klosterman would like to thank the following individuals for their assistance, insight, and support throughout the writing and editing of *I Wear the Black Hat*:

Melissa Maerz
Dmitry Kiper
Brant Rumble
Daniel Greenberg
Rob Sheffield
Bob Ethington
Jon Dolan
Michael Weinreb
Zach Baron
Brian Raftery
Ben Heller
John Jeremiah Sullivan
Steve Marsh
Sean Howe
Bill Simmons
Dan Fierman
Susan Moldow
Nan Graham
Kate Lloyd
Elisa Rivlin

Index

INDEX

INDEX

INDEX

INDEX

INDEX

INDEX

INDEX

"Suicide Solution" (Osbourne), 156
"Sultans of Swing" (Dire Straits), 29
Sunan Abu Dawud (Muhammad), 55
Super Bowl, 95, 97, 98
"Sweet Lew" (Pearl Jam), 172–73
Swift, Taylor, 35–37

"Take It Easy" (Eagles), 23–24, 26
Tangents Within a Framework (Page), 159
Tarantino, Quentin, 87, 149
Tatum, Jack, 101–02
Taylor, James, 150
television series
    drug dealers portrayed in, 47–50
    public opinion on quality of, 46–47
    See also specific series and networks
terrorist attacks (9/11/2001), 55–56, 161
Texas Rangers, 195
Thelema religion, 158
They Call Me Assassin (Tatum), 102
They Still Call Me Assassin (Tatum), 102
Thicke, Alan, 28
Thomson, Judith Jarvis, 146
"Thrilla in Manila" (Ali-Frazier fight, 1971), 51, 52
Time (magazine), 197
Tone Lōc, 93
Torre, Joe, 197
Tosh, Daniel, 83
To the Limit (Eliot), 25
Tramell, Catherine (fictional character, *Basic Instinct*), 111–12
Travolta, John, 80
Tripp, Linda, 115, 121–22, 125, 126
Tuchman, Gary, 55
Turner, Kathleen, 112
TV Guide, 46
Twilight (film), 194
Twitter, 60, 160, 161, 163

2 Live Crew, 78
Tyson, Mike, 60

Ugly Betty (TV series), 193
"Under My Thumb" (Rolling Stones), 150
"Under the Bridge" (Red Hot Chili Peppers), 30
Under the Gaslight (play), 10
Untergang, Der (film), 193
Urban Outfitters, 33
USA Today, 195
USFL, 98
US Weekly, 36
U2, 33

Vader, Darth (character, *Star Wars*), 7
Van Halen, 28–29
"veil of ignorance" concept, 4
Verducci, Tom, 197
Verhoeven, Paul, 111
Very Best of the Eagles, The (CD), 26
VH1, 134
Vietcong, 54
Vietnam War, 52, 108, 145
vigilantism
    Death Wish (film) and, 66–69
    Goetz's subway attack and, 60, 63–66, 73–75
Village Voice, 60
villains and villainy
    Ali-Frazier boxing matches and, 50–54
    Assange and WikiLeaks and, 143–45
    Clinton's affair and, 114–15, 125–27
    con artists as, 42–43
    D. B. Cooper's airplane hijacking and, 40–42, 54–55, 56–57
    Death Wish (film) and, 66–69
    drug dealers in television shows and, 47–50

213